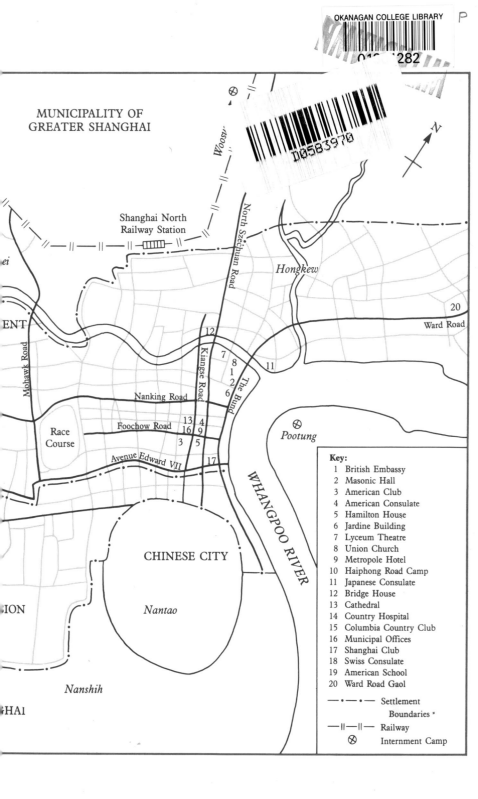

MUNICIPALITY OF
GREATER SHANGHAI

N

Woosu-

North Szechuan Road

Shanghai North
Railway Station

ei

Hongkew

ENT

20

Ward Road

Mohawk Road

12

7

8

1

2

6

11

The Bund

Kiangse Road

Nanking Road

Pootung

Race
Course

Foochow Road

13 4

16 9

3   5

Avenue Edward VII

17

WHANGPOO RIVER

CHINESE CITY

Nantao

ION

Nanshih

HAI

Key:

1 British Embassy
2 Masonic Hall
3 American Club
4 American Consulate
5 Hamilton House
6 Jardine Building
7 Lyceum Theatre
8 Union Church
9 Metropole Hotel
10 Haiphong Road Camp
11 Japanese Consulate
12 Bridge House
13 Cathedral
14 Country Hospital
15 Columbia Country Club
16 Municipal Offices
17 Shanghai Club
18 Swiss Consulate
19 American School
20 Ward Road Gaol

—·—·— Settlement
             Boundaries ²

—‖—‖— Railway

⊗   Internment Camp

CAPTIVE IN SHANGHAI

	DATE DUE		
MR.8/10			

CAPTIVE IN SHANGHAI

HUGH COLLAR

Abridged by Pauline Woodroffe
With an Introduction by Kerrie L. MacPherson

HONG KONG
OXFORD UNIVERSITY PRESS
OXFORD NEW YORK
1990

Oxford University Press

Oxford New York Toronto
Petaling Jaya Singapore Hong Kong Tokyo
Delhi Bombay Calcutta Madras Karachi
Nairobi Dar es Salaam Cape Town
Melbourne Auckland

and associated companies in
Berlin Ibadan

First published 1990
Published in the United States
by Oxford University Press, Inc., New York

British Library Cataloguing in Publication Data
Collar. Hugh
Captive in Shanghai: a story of internment in World War
II.
I. China. British prisoners of war. 1939–1945 —
Biographies
I. Title II. Woodroffe. Pauline
940.547252

ISBN 0-19-585004-1

Library of Congress Cataloging-in-Publication Data available

Printed in Hong Kong by Liang Yu Printing Fty. Ltd.
Published by Oxford University Press, Warwick House, Hong Kong

ACKNOWLEDGEMENTS

Hugh Collar's family would like to express their thanks to all those who eventually persuaded him to agree to the publication of this account, and especially to Mr J. Ford who persisted in the location of a publisher. Also to Tess Johnston and Kerrie L. MacPherson for their help with the map of Shanghai, and to Mr John McAulay, who spent so much time verifying information and providing the map of the camp — with help from other fellow internees.

All photographs come from the family collection except for: Refugees from outlying areas crowding into the International Settlement (*China Quarterly*, 1937); Crowds of refugees throng the Bund (Randall Gould, *The China Journal*, September 1937). Photographs of the author's armband and the Christmas card were taken by Lime Tree Studios, Sevenoaks, Kent.

ABRIDGER'S NOTE

T HIS is the story, told by himself, of the wartime experiences of Hubert Collar CBE, 1900–1985.

When the Japanese occupied the Shanghai International Settlement in December 1941, Hugh Collar was a Director of Imperial Chemical Industries (ICI) in Shanghai. Having been Chairman of the British Residents' Association since 1940, he soon found himself head of the British community. He faced grim and unforeseen problems and tackled them with amazing initiative, courage, and an invaluable sense of humour.

He had to fight a battle of wits against the Japanese authorities, who held him personally responsible for the actions of any member of the sizeable community. He also organized relief for British residents who were almost destitute, and tried to shield civilians from the threat of sudden imprisonment and torture — a regime which he vividly describes.

It was clearly only a matter of time before Collar himself, together with the rest of the British community, would be interned. When this happened, he found himself chief representative of some three hundred and sixty internees deemed 'prominent persons' or 'dangerous criminals' who were wretchedly housed and cut off from communication with their relations 'for the duration'. How, trapped between 'The upper millstone of the Japanese and the lower millstone of the body of the camp', he strove to protect his charges, and how they managed to maintain some semblance of civilized life in conditions of great hardship, is the crux of his story.

Collar wrote this account during the period of indefinite leave he was given by his Company after the Japanese surrender. As he wrote later:

Four years of daily contact with the Japanese had left me somewhat frazzled. Not quite a nervous wreck, but definitely not easy to live with. This was what decided me to try to write it out of my system. I can well remember the sigh of relief with which I wrote the last few words on a storm tossed freighter on the way back to Shanghai. The exercise worked.

The account was never intended for publication, and it was not until Collar was in his eighties that he was persuaded of its worth. As part of an active retirement, after many years working to improve trade relations between England, China, and Japan, he was Honorary Secretary to the China Society. Council members of the Society much regretted that their Annual General Meeting in July 1985 was the last he attended. His remarkable buoyancy endeared him to all members. He gave me a copy of the manuscript at that last meeting, asking me if I would reorganize it. This I have done in a slightly abridged version in the belief that there is much of interest and inspiration for present-day readers in his modest but absorbing report.

In the Romanization of Chinese names and terms, the traditional renditions used by foreigners living in Shanghai at the time have been used. In addition, for key Chinese figures, the Wade-Giles equivalent of the name is given in brackets.

MRS P. W. WOODROFFE

INTRODUCTION

On the eve of the Greater East Asian War (1937–45), Shanghai had achieved unparalleled leadership as China's premier financial, commercial and industrial centre, and was one of the world's busiest international ports. Shanghai also functioned as one of the primary if not in many regards as the chief political and cultural node. With a population hovering close to four million, it had become one of the most populous cities in the world — in a class with New York, London, and Tokyo. Furthermore this salient rank was achieved and suffered within a scant 100 years — a brief period, particularly by previous Chinese standards. What is in fact revealed by the raw statistics of growth, is a measure of 'modernization' which in its Chinese context is as dramatic, though it has been less well attended, as the 'modernization' of Meiji Japan.

Underlying this salience were the meldings of Chinese and Western — mainly British — efforts to lay down what became the infrastructures requisite for the city's survival in the face of its astonishing expansion and rise to pre-eminence. These efforts commenced with Shanghai's opening to foreign trade in 1843 at the conclusion of the first Anglo-Chinese War (Opium War) and the signing of the Treaty of Nanking.

If some enthusiastic observers wished to gild Shanghai's future by depicting it as the 'gateway to China', as the entrepôt for the abundance of the Yangtze Basin, or as a natural magnet for international commerce, such observations stemmed more from romance than realism. For the people of Shanghai dwelled amid sinuous, regularly silted watercourses, settled upon the residues of 750,000 square miles of interior drainage on mud flats more than a hundred metres deep. Living an uncomfortable distance from open sea in an area devoid of readily accessible industrial raw materials, they were trying to prosper in close proximity to established competitors in Hangchow, Ningpo, Soochow, and Nanking. Given such an environment, it would have been difficult to predict that Shanghai's designation as a treaty port by the Ch'ing government, with British and American settlement rights and followed by the French concession five years later, would eventually afford China such a centre for development.

By mutual agreement of the Taotai, Kung Moo Kew (Kung Mu-chiu) and the British Consul, Captain G. Balfour, a site was set aside for foreign residence a short distance from the walled city and its suburbs, and was embodied in the original Land Regulations of 1845. Under these regulations, British subjects could acquire land, rent or sell properties, and with the creation of the Roads and Jetties Committee, a rudimentary government was constituted with a municipal code of sorts. But Chinese and British assumptions underlying these regulations, namely that the settlements would exclude Chinese from residence and that all other nationals would agree to the regulations as construed by the British consul, proved unworkable. With the devastation wrought by the Small Sword and Taiping Rebellions during the 1850s and 1860s driving an estimated one million refugees into the safety of the settlements, and the inability of the Ch'ing government to provide protection for the community, the Shanghai Municipal Council was created in 1854. Based on revised Land Regulations, the SMC constituted a body of representatives elected by ratepayers, with the authority to organize a common police force and exercise compulsory powers of taxation. The events of the 1850s also led to the development of a special doctrine that would figure so prominently in the subsequent history of Shanghai. The foreign community, under the 'law of self-preservation', claimed the right to defence, to armed neutrality in Chinese civil wars, and to the exclusion of Chinese armed forces within the settlement.

Thus the main configurations of Shanghai's nineteenth- and twentieth-century development were formed. The Americans eventually amalgamated their 'settlement' with the British, but the French, after some hesitation, rejected the revised Land Regulations and created a separate *conseil* in 1862 for the administration of the French Concession. In turn each area was overwhelmingly populated by Chinese.

Shanghai now came under the same scrutiny effectually focused on major communities abroad. Such scrutiny, exercised especially by foreigners, essentially meant that provisions for public health, public order, housing, justice, governance and administration, communications and transport, markets, cultural amenities, educational facilities, and the like, even in the form of marginally effective technologies, were deemed basic to the survival, let alone future prosperity of the city. These massive efforts to emplace the urban infrastructure, albeit sometimes slow and fumbling — though hardly less so than in large foreign cities themselves — left indelible marks. Even visually, the city skyline and industrial prominences registered foreign imprimaturs. As H.E. Arnold, British

Chairman of the SMC in 1930 mused, 'the Bund ... in the early morning, with its huge buildings and waterfront, with the outline of ships gradually taking shape and emerging from the morning mist, is reminiscent of the Embankment in London'.

By the turn of the century, however, Shanghai's Chinese, for many reasons — some politico-military, many of them economic — were eager to participate in international trade and finance. They were also ripe for making their contributions towards, as well as borrowing from, foreign urban experiences that seemed to light a better path to modernity. Between 1898 and 1912, they initiated and sustained efforts both to create their own municipal council candidly modelled on the SMC, and to grapple with the essentials of urban existence. By the 1920s, the Chinese in the foreign settlements, through persistent pressure by their numerous and densely reticulated guilds, chambers of commerce, ratepayer and land interests, forced the Shanghai Municipal Council to grant Chinese representation on the council. More importantly, the walled city and the proto-municipalities of Nanshih and Chapei, along with other areas surrounding the foreign settlements, were forged into one municipality in 1927, directly subordinated to the Administrative Yuan of the Nationalist government, with the promulgation of China's first municipal law. This Municipality of Greater Shanghai was established in order to make coherent the Chinese urban administration as well as to raise the infrastructural development of these areas up to the standards extant within the foreign settlements. But that was not the sum of the matter. A new generation of reformers, heirs to Dr Sun Yat-sen's republican revolution, conceived of the Greater Shanghai Plan, a visionary scheme for rebuilding the city centre in Kiangwan as an adjunct to new port facilities (long sought by the SMC), in order to afford Shanghai the room in which to continue to develop and prosper. In addition, it would allow for the eventual rendition of the foreign settlements to Chinese control with minimal disruption to trade and foreign investment.

In recognition of these realities and the gradual weakening of the British position in China (although the British would continue to hold the largest share of China's foreign trade), in 1930 the SMC commissioned the Hon. Justice Feetham to prepare a report on the 'present position and prospects' of foreign Shanghai. Though positive towards the promising developments in the Chinese administration of Greater Shanghai and cognizant of the restrictions placed on any future physical or political expansion of the self-governing settlements, the *Report* cautioned against any immediate changes to their status on several grounds. Firstly, that

the Chinese Nationalist government at Nanking was unable to maintain
unity in the face of powerful regional war-lords and the increasing pressure
of a growing communist party; and secondly, the expansion of Japanese
interests on the Chinese mainland.

Acknowledging the wisdom of such a view, but unable to reconcile
it with the reality of the Chinese desire for the resumption of sovereignty
over the settlements, a new scheme was floated by several long-term
British residents in Shanghai. One of these was Arthur de Carle Sowerby,
explorer, naturalist, artist, founder of *The China Journal* and later to spend
the Pacific War interned in a Japanese concentration camp. Sowerby,
writing in the *Journal* in 1932, proposed the elimination of the 'old system
of multiple authority' and the unification of the entire city, thus creating
a ' "Greater Shanghai" with a charter from the Chinese Government
for a period of twenty-five to thirty years, ruled by a District Council
on which both Chinese and foreigners would be adequately represented
. . . and protected by a demilitarized zone'. But Sowerby's civil call
for a 'Comity of Nations' came at a time when Shanghai's fate was
increasingly framed by Japanese ambitions in China. These included a
'New Order' or 'Asia for the Asiatics', a Greater East Asian Co-Prosperity
Sphere, the establishment of a client state of Manchukuo in the Chinese
province of Manchuria, and eventual hegemony over China.

Initially the Japanese presence in Shanghai was confined to a few small
business enterprises, such as porcelain import-export, medicine, coal,
printing, antiques, and sundries. It was not until the conclusion of the
Sino-Japanese War of 1894–5 and the signing of the Treaty of
Shimonoseki, which gave Japan most-favoured-nation status, that the
Japanese community developed. By 1915, with the Western powers
preoccupied in Europe with the First World War, Japan had seized the
opportunity to pursue their interests in China aggressively, by presenting
the Chinese government with the 'Twenty-one Demands' as well as
occupying the former German concessions in Shantung. Gaining
confidence from such actions, and lured by the stability and prosperity
of the foreign settlements, Japanese business in Shanghai flourished and
the Japanese population soon greatly exceeded all other foreign nationals,
by 1930 numbering over 18,000, double the British population as
recorded by the SMC census.

The Japanese community, located principally in Hongkew — dubbed
'Little Tokyo', — remained at least nominally integrated into the larger
foreign settlements under the supervision of the Shanghai Municipal
Council, a situation unique to Japanese concessions in China. Their

enclave, north of Soochow creek, did not evince the grand colonial style of the British Taipans or traders, replete with clubs, cricket matches, and the inevitable racecourse. The community was more modest and self-contained and its denizens, outside of a small élite, were predominately drawn from the lower middle classes. Unlike the Chinese residents of the settlements before 1926, however, the Japanese ratepayers, by virtue of their treaty rights, were represented on the Municipal Council. They would, reflecting their growing influence and power within the community as well as in China generally, demand an ever-increasing voice in the administration of Shanghai.

Yet the context had changed. During the 1920s and 1930s from Shanghai emerged the revolutionary political and cultural consciousness of a new generation of Chinese. The security of the settlements fostered both the May Fourth Movement (1919) with its emphasis on remaking China free from imperialism and strong in its advocacy of 'science' and 'democracy', and the founding of the Communist Party in 1921. While over the radio 'Little Miss Shanghai' blared out the hourly stock market index, radical intellectual journals, advocating a bewildering variety of 'isms', with titles such as 'New Youth', 'New Women', and 'New Tide', as well as a prolific popular press, kept Shanghai's urbanites informed. Shanghai also became a haven to new political refugees — Russians fleeing from the Bolshevik revolution, and a sizeable Jewish population in the 1930s. Gangsters and adventurers seeking safe harbour and rich pickings gravitated to Shanghai. Reflecting such a volatile political and cultural milieu, the more unsavoury aspects of Shanghai's big city reputation gained prominence.

Japan, in 1932, in seeking to achieve its dreams in China, helped to destroy Shanghai's. With horrific effect, the Chinese-administered areas of Shanghai, including the new city centre under construction at Kiangwan, were bombed in retaliation for the growing anti-Japanese nationalism of the Chinese. This nationalism was expressed in proliferating and effective boycotts and strikes aimed at the principal Japanese industry of cotton textiles. By 1931 these activities had brought Japanese commerce at Shanghai and other treaty ports to a virtual standstill.

The foreign settlements, constrained by the Land Regulations, and by the power struggles between the Chinese and Japanese representatives on the SMC, maintained a shaky 'neutrality' in the face of increasing hostility between the two protagonists. The Shanghai Volunteer Corps, originally established to protect the settlements from both the Taiping rebels and the Imperial forces of the 1850s, proved inadequate to this fresh challenge and were temporarily supported by British and smaller numbers of American and French troops. Yet, it fell upon the shoulders of the remarkably adept Mayor of Greater Shanghai, Wu Te-chen (Wu T'ieh-ch'eng) to negotiate a bitter truce, at the same time rebuilding the ruined portions of the old and new city as well as preparing for future military engagements with the Japanese. In turn, the Japanese presence in Shanghai was augmented by sizeable military and naval forces, and the violation of the traditional neutrality of the settlements by the Japanese Naval Landing Party effectively put the Hongkew district, as well as the Chinese-administered area contiguous to it, under Japanese control.

In the brief hiatus before the outbreak of the Greater East Asian War, despite the adverse circumstances of civil war, famine, and floods, Shanghai continued to progress and to grow. It was said that while bullets whistled overhead, Shanghai's construction workers were 'keeping pace with the tempo of machine guns and were pouring cement and raising steel'. However, Shanghai's strength was its undoing. For no army, as the Japanese well understood, could conquer China without first capturing its economic heart.

For a time after the invasion of Shanghai in 1937 and the setting up of the Japanese puppet regime in the Greater Shanghai municipality, life in the foreign settlements, though guarded and restrained, continued. But Japanese commandeering of the foreign settlements was merely a matter of time. At the outbreak of the Pacific War in 1941, the British heads of the municipal departments 'resigned' and were replaced by their Japanese deputies. All British and American influence was to be expunged from Shanghai. To that end, Britons, Americans, and other enemy nationals who were perceived as 'dangerous' either because of their positions in the community or by association, were interned in one of three concentration camps built for that purpose: Lunghua, south of the city; Pootung across the Whangpoo opposite the Bund; and the Haiphong Road camp located in the western district of the city. But it was in a former apartment house and hotel in Hongkew that the Japanese Kempeitai conducted their notorious interrogations and torture of Chinese and 'enemy' nationals. H. G. W. Woodhead, journalist for over forty years in China, and editor of *Oriental Affairs*, called it the 'infamy of Bridge House', having barely survived three months' imprisonment within its walls. Indeed others would survive the terrors and afflictions of the camps and remember the shadow that fell over this great city. Hugh Collar was one.

Yet, from an historian's perspective, Hugh Collar's story constitutes more than just memory and survival. Placed in a larger context it parallels the survival of a great city in the face of adversity. Among the different kinds of historical time, the Japanese invasion can be understood as a short but brutal interlude in the more enduring rhythm of Shanghai's urban evolution.

From the vantage point of 1893, the fiftieth anniversary of the opening of Shanghai to foreign trade, the entire polyglot community celebrated the transformation of Shanghai into an international city. Among the widespread praise for past efforts and ebullience over future prospects, one celebrant remarked: 'We may try and fancy to ourselves what Shanghai will be like fifty years hence, and imagine how 1943 will be observed.'

None could foresee that Shanghai's centenary would arrive in the midst of the terrible events of the Second World War. But celebrated it was, for in 1943, Britain and America, signatories to the Treaty of Nanking, relinquished their special rights and interests to the Chinese Nationalist government in Chungking. The foreign settlements had ceased to exist. The birth of a unified Greater Shanghai would now command the future.

KERRIE L. MACPHERSON

BIBLIOGRAPHY

Barber, Noel, *The Fall of Shanghai* (New York, Coward, McCann & Geohagan, 1979).

Clague, Peter, *Bridge House: The True Story of a Shanghai Chamber of Horrors* (Hong Kong, South China Morning Post, 1983).

Duus, Peter, Myers, Ramon H., and Peattie, Mark R. (eds.), *The Japanese Informal Empire in China 1895-1937* (Princeton, Princeton University Press, 1989).

Feetham, Richard, *Report of the Hon. Richard Feetham, CMG to the Shanghai Municipal Council* (4 vols.) (Shanghai, *North-China Daily News and Herald* Office, 1931).

MacPherson, K.L., A Wilderness of Marshes: *The Origins of Public Health in Shanghai, 1843-1893* (Hong Kong, Oxford University Press, 1987).

____'Designing China's Urban Future: The Greater Shanghai Plan, 1927-1937', *Planning Perspectives*, Vol. 5, 1990, pp. 39-62.

Smith, Dean (comp.), 'Nutrition in Civilian Internment Camps in the Far East, January 1942-August 1945', *Dean Smith Papers*, London School of Tropical Medicine (n.d.).

Sowerby, Arthur de C., 'Greater Shanghai', *The China Journal*, Vol. XVI No. 5, pp. 215-17, May 1932.

Sturton, Stephen D., *From Mission Hospital to Concentration Camp* (London, Marshall, Morgan and Scott, 1949).

The Jubilee of Shanghai 1843-1893. Shanghai: Past and Present, and a Full Account of the Proceedings on the 17th and 18th November, 1893 (Shanghai, *North-China Daily News* Office, 1893).

CONTENTS

PLATES

MAPS

1
THE JAPANESE PRESENCE

LIFE in China had certainly not been pleasant for the foreigner since 1937. We, the British in Shanghai, fondly imagined that if war was declared against the Japanese our cut and dried plans for the winding up of our business and personal affairs would be put into effect. We imagined that evacuation ships would be brought nearer and as matters progressed to their well-ordered conclusion, we should all sail away. Ultimatums would then be presented and the war could begin. The reality, however, was far otherwise.

In Hongkew, the northern portion of the International Settlement at Shanghai, the Japanese population had increased with disturbing speed until they outnumbered the European and American inhabitants by ten to one. Up to 1940, the government of the Settlement had been pretty much a closed corporation. The members of the Shanghai Municipal Council (SMC), were predominately British, with a leavening of Americans. As time passed, it had been found expedient to admit two Japanese, a non-British European, and finally some Chinese, but the balance of control remained with the British and European members. Voting powers were vested in ratepayers above a certain assessed rateability. There was a plurality of voting, whereby the owners of property had a vote for each property which they owned, or each tenant for each property occupied.

Under the 'Land Regulations', the original constitution of the Settlement by which a piece of wasteland was set aside for the sole purposeful use of the Western Barbarians, no Chinese was permitted to own land therein. But the Chinese found it a most desirable place in which to live. To own land is the primary aim of every Chinese who has laboriously been able to ring one dollar against another, and what more desirable place was there in the whole of China in which to own land, than in the Shanghai Settlement. Ownership was secure and values were steadily increasing. So the Chinese bought land, and because they could not own it officially, the Deeds were registered in the names of

British and American business men, solicitors, estate agents and insurance companies. As the registered owners, these business men had the voting rights inherent in the ownership of each piece of property, with the result that they exercised the Chinese vote, acting as trustees for the real owners.

The majority of the Chinese did not object to this; far from it. It was the British and American control of the Settlement which gave the land its value and security. Several of these nominal owners were, by this means, enabled to exercise hundreds of votes, and by and large a relatively small group was able to control the municipal elections.

The Japanese, cock-a-hoop over their 'victories' in China, felt that their numerical superiority in Shanghai ought to give them control of municipal affairs. We felt that our greater financial investment should be considered of at least equal weight. We also believed that their recent large increase in numbers resulted from a deliberate policy on the part of their Government, and did not justify a sweeping overthrow of the traditional set up in which there were separate and independent British and American Settlements. We had, moreover, had ample evidence of the treatment which Chinese were receiving at the hands of Japan, and we had no intention whatsoever of placing the million odd Chinese who lived in the Settlement under Japanese control. Some were our friends, nearly all were in some form or other contributing to our long established and valuable trade with China.

So the Japanese decided to beat us at our own game, in reverse. Whereas our large voting power resulted from numerous ownerships, large and small, they conceived the bright idea of nominally subdividing their holdings. Previously it had been the practice for owners of buildings to pay municipal taxes themselves, and to collect pro rata shares from their tenants as part of the rent, so that the landlord retained voting power. The Japanese now reversed the process and arranged for all tenants whose rental assessment was sufficiently large to qualify for a vote, to pay municipal taxes direct and to register themselves as qualified voters. The numbers of Matsumotos and Fujiyamas on the voting list grew rapidly to alarming proportions, and it was soon realized that the British-American vote was in danger of being completely swamped.

It did not require a very lengthy investigation to uncover the Japanese plan, and to concert measures to counter it. In the greatest secrecy, British and American properties were subdivided in a similar way, and even in ways that the Japanese had not dreamed of. These new voting powers were, by arrangement, dumped on the Registrar at the latest possible moment before the 1938 municipal elections, so that the Japanese were confronted with a *fait accompli*, with no time for a counter attack, just when they thought they were going to have everything their own way. To say that they were enraged would be putting it mildly.

The elections were held. The British-American group did not utilize their overwhelming new voting power to throw out the Japanese candidates, but merely to maintain the status quo, allowing two Japanese to be elected as usual. Nevertheless, the Japanese were not appeased, they had lost face, particularly in the eyes of the Chinese, and they chose a typically Japanese way of showing it.

The elections were followed by the Annual General Meeting of ratepayers. This was usually a sedate and sparsely attended ceremony. However, it was felt that no hall could possibly hold the crowd that would turn up and it was therefore held in the Race Course in the centre of the town. The ratepayers were accommodated in the Grand Stand, mat sheds were built facing the stands, and a platform was erected therein on which the councillors were seated and from which speeches could be made. Elaborate precautions were taken to ensure that only registered voters were admitted. It was known that every Japanese voter who could stand on his feet would be forced to attend, and special measures were therefore taken to urge the British and American voters to turn up in force.

The Japanese arrived early, and seated themselves in a solid phalanx opposite the southern end of the councillors' mat shed. There was tension in the air, but proceedings opened relatively quietly.

Motions were put and in one case, where a show of hands was obviously too close, the voters left their seats and entered aye and nay enclosures where an accurate count could be made. A further motion was put. The head of the Japanese Residents Association made an impassioned speech which evoked angry shouts of enthusiasm from his supporters. There was relative quiet whilst his speech was translated. The motion was then put to the vote on a show of hands.

Then came the bloomer. The Danish Consul-General, Dean of the Consular Corps, and as such, traditionally chairman of these meetings, declared the motion carried on the show of hands, where a count should obviously have been called for. There was immediate uproar. Mr W. J. Keswick, Chairman of the Municipal Council, rose to speak. During the confusion, the head of the Japanese Residents Association had left his seat in the stands, and crossed to the platform. As Mr Keswick approached the microphone, he reached the platform, pulled a gun from his pocket, shouted something unintelligible and fired. The scene that followed was one that those present will not easily forget.

Mr Keswick staggered and put his hand to his back, but he was damned if he would give the Japanese the satisfaction of seeing him fall. He turned back towards his seat whilst his assailant was being disarmed. The Japanese section rose to its feet with a roar, those in front plunged across the space separating them from the platform, whilst those behind and above threw everything they could lay their hands on at the occupants of the platform. Cushions, wooden seat covers, chairs and even cameras, went flying through the air. The Shanghai Municipal Police got to the platform first, held the steps, and then managed to form a line across the space between the platform and the stands, and the battle began. There was fortunately no more shooting, and the police contented themselves with trying to hold back the enraged horde of Japanese whilst the councillors and their wounded chairman were hustled out of the back of their stand through a hole torn in the matting, and escorted away to safety.

With the departure of their intended victims, the maelstrom slowly subsided. The meeting found itself dissolved and the voters went back to offices and homes through a downpour of rain. Mr Keswick recovered. The head of the Japanese Residents Association was handed over to his own authorities for punishment.

So! We did not like Japanese ideas on municipal government. They were, of course, not beaten or even discouraged. They simply set about to get by foul means what they could not get by fair. They interfered to such an extent with municipal administration, particularly policing in the Hongkew area, that it had virtually to be abandoned to them. This area, north of the Soochow Creek, in which the great bulk of the Japanese lived, also constituted the principal industrial area of the town, and included most of the foreign-owned factories, wharves and goaowns. In this area their word became law, and their law was not order. Their favourite phrase, the 'New Order in East Asia', was more frequently referred to as the 'New Odour'!

Japanese business was not good. Much of Shanghai industry lay in processing raw materials, or preparing native goods for export. These were, of course, obtained from the Chinese in the Hinterland. But for some reason, the Chinese did not appear to appreciate the benefits of trading with the Japanese. They actually had the effrontery to refuse to sell their goods to them. This was met by simple confiscation, but the

Chinese found ways and means to sell their goods to other nationals, and not all goods of course came from Japanese controlled territory, so that there was still a fair flow of material towards Shanghai in non-Japanese hands; enough at least to keep the wheels of commerce turning. Most of these goods had to go through the Hongkew area, either for processing, or enroute to the wharves. What more simple than to hijack the goods straight off the streets, trucks, coolies and all. The S.M. police could not protect them as they were practically driven off the streets, except, of course, the Japanese members of the force, who could be relied on to play their appropriate part. So British and American trade in the Hongkew area suffered further heavy losses and became a shadow of its former self.

There was of course still the area south of the creek. The line of the creek provided a natural geographic barrier, and without the backing of their naval and military forces, whose barracks were all in the Hongkew area, the Japanese did not feel quite strong enough to attempt to exercise overt control. But to the west of the settlement lay the Jessfield area, part of the Chinese municipality, which provided an ideal base for infiltration into the Settlement.

Armed robbery, abduction, kidnapping, and political murder had always been recognized forms of commerce in China. Shanghai was no exception, although these were normally kept pretty well in hand by the efforts of the police forces which, in both the International Settlement and the French Concession, were almost entirely officered by Europeans. The Japanese now set about organizing Chinese gangs in a big way and in particular, gave them protective boltholes in the Jessfield area. The most notorious of these was 91 Jessfield Road, just outside the Settlement boundary. Here the Japanese established Gendarmerie Headquarters for the western area, and it also became the principal hideout for the gangs which they controlled.

Then began an organized reign of terror. Newspapers which expressed any pro-Nationalist or anti-Japanese sentiments were bombed again and again. Nationalist sympathizers were abducted in the streets or shot down in cold blood. Elaborate gambling halls were set up in the western area which soon earned and justified their sobriquet of 'Bad Lands'. There were many running gun battles in the streets, and numerous policemen and passers-by were killed or wounded. The gangsters had only to melt into the crowd and cross the border to gain the security of the Japanese controlled areas, and if a few were caught and spilled the beans, those higher up could not be touched. Protests to the Japanese were met with bland professions of ignorance, or absolute denials. Violence held sway. This was the state of affairs in Shanghai on the 7 December 1941. It is not surprising that the news of Pearl Harbor was a very nasty blow. We had virtually abandoned hope that the Japanese would in any way recognize the international character of the Settlement, and the thought of being left entirely in their hands was most disquieting.

2

THE BRITISH RESIDENTS'
ASSOCIATION

I PERSONALLY was particularly unhappy about the prospect of Shanghai in Japanese hands. I was then Chairman of the British Residents' Association, and anyone who was prominent politically was likely to be very much *persona non grata* with the Japanese.

I had not taken part in public life prior to 1939. In a large company such as ICI, with offices in all the main trading centres throughout China, staff were moved about a fair amount. In general one was seldom able to settle down in any particular place long enough to feel either the desire or the need for taking an extensive part in public life. I had spent the whole of the period between 1934 and 1938 in Shanghai and on my return there from home leave at the end of 1938 it looked as though I might reasonably expect to stay there for a further spell. In 1939 I was made a Director of the Company.

In September of that same year, Germany invaded Poland and England declared war on Germany. In 1940 Japan joined the Axis and the possibility of her entering the war on the side of Germany increased. In the early Spring of that year, V. St. J. Killery, Vice-Chairman of my company, retired to England to join the Ministry of Economic Warfare. He was replaced by G.A. Haley. Killery had been a member of the Shanghai Municipal Council and Haley was co-opted to take his place. Haley had until then been a member of the committee of the British Residents' Association, but since he felt it was undesirable that he should serve on both these boards, he resigned from his position in the B.R.A. As he thought it good policy for our company to be represented on the committee of the B.R.A. in view of our large foreign staff and wide business interests, he suggested that either C.B. Cook or myself should offer ourselves for co-option in his place.

At this time I knew nobody outside my small circle of friends and immediate business acquaintances and I felt that as a member of the board of the company I ought to take some small part in public life in order to have an opportunity to become better known. As Cyril Cook was already well known, it was decided that I should go on to the B.R.A. committee, subject of course to my candidature being approved.

Haley's proposal that I be co-opted in his place was accepted, and in the summer of 1940 I found myself a member of the general committee of the B.R.A. Although I did not realize it then, that was the beginning of four years of hard work, fear and excitement.

The Committee was large, consisting of about twenty people, and for the first few meetings I said little. I was by some years the youngest member, and was certainly the greenest so far as public service was concerned. I had never made a speech in my life, and it required all my courage to open my mouth at all in what was to me a most august assembly.

The British Residents' Association had been founded some years earlier as a means of placing a correct expression of the views of the British residents in China before Parliament in London, as opposed to the previous procedure of reliance solely on the Consular authorities. It was felt that the Consular authorities were frequently too much bound up in red tape and that their views were too often coloured by expediency to give a true reflection of the views of the average resident. Their recommendations or reports could not fail to be influenced at times by the thought that a particular line of action might give them personally a great deal of trouble, or that the need to adopt a stiff attitude *vis-à-vis* the Chinese authorities on one matter might prejudice the successful outcome of another. The Association started off with a blaze of enthusiasm, with the main body in Shanghai, and branch organizations in all the larger outports. Such an organization cannot of course be kept at fever heat, and interest in its activities, and correspondingly its membership, fluctuated. Although it never became moribund, there were long periods during which its activities could only be described as humdrum. The outbreak of war in September 1939 immediately provided a new *raison d'être*, and the B.R.A. became a centre of patriotic endeavour on the part of British Nationals in China. When I joined the committee, their widespread programme of national effort, particularly in the form of organized financial contributions, was already well under way.

After I had been on the committee for about three months, during which I did little and said less, the Annual General Meeting came round, and the elections for the General Committee for the coming year were held. When the votes were counted, it was found that J.R. Jones topped the bill, I was a few votes behind, and H.E. Arnhold, one of the prime movers in the organization and Chairman for several years, had not even been re-elected. I was naturally pleased that I had polled so many votes since it would not have suprised me in the least if I had been thrown out. After all, I had merely been co-opted to fill a vacancy and had done nothing to justify such support. The only explanation I could think of was that I focused attention by being a completely new face on the platform.

A few days later, I was enjoying my usual Tuesday game of bowls in the alleys at the Shanghai Club. I had started playing a year or so before, and was just beginning to knock up a good score now and then. We did not usually have many spectators and I was a little surprised when W.J. Hawkings walked in and sat down, since so far as I knew he wasn't a player himself and took no interest in the game. After I had finished my turn he beckoned me over.

'You know we are in a bit of a fix over chairmanship of the B.R.A. this year since Arnhold hasn't been elected?'

'Yes, I suppose you are, although I haven't thought very much about it. There are a number of the old members of the committee still on it, and what about J.R. Jones? He topped the poll.'

'It isn't quite so simple as that. Several of us have been talking it over and we believe that the failure of the voters to re-elect Arnhold is an indication that they are tired of what they feel is the 'old gang' and they want new blood. We have thought it over very carefully, and we think you are the most suitable person for the job.'

'What job?' said I, quite unable to believe Hawkings meant what it sounded like.

'Chairman, of course.' I must have looked as I felt, completely dumbfounded, for he continued: 'Don't look so surprised. After all you were almost at the top of the poll. J.R. Jones is not anxious to serve, and agrees that you are the man. You musn't think that I am making the suggestion without careful enquiries having first been made from people who know you.'

'But nobody knows me', I replied.

'Don't worry about that. Enough people know you to satisfy us. Take time to think it over if you like, but let me know by tomorrow evening if you can.'

It was my turn to bowl again. I pulled myself together determined to bowl a 'Strike' to show my command of myself. I didn't. I finished and dropped back to Hawkings. The more I protested the more he took the line that I could and should take the job. I finally said that I would let him know. It was too big a thing to agree to right away.

There was just one more thing. Hawkings had assurance of support from only half the committee. He had not talked to them all, and probably would not do so. He said that it would therefore be necessary for me to vote for myself. I did not like that part of it a bit. It sounded rather unsporting to me.

The most important person to consult was Haley, Chairman of my company, and the cause of all the trouble. The job was liable to take up a lot of time both in and out of the office. I shall not forget his advice and warning:

'Take it on if you feel like it, but remember two things. First, that you are in ICI and people will always connect you with the company, so that whatever you do is going to reflect on the company. Secondly, you must be prepared for the fact that you are going to make a lot of enemies. An organization such as the B.R.A. cannot avoid doing things which will be unpopular with some people in the community. It is impossible to please all the people all the time. You personally will fall heir to the ill feeling caused by unpopular actions of the Association.'

Before an enraged populace could get to me, it so happened that the Japanese locked me up *in medias res*. Perhaps I should be grateful for that.

I decided, not without a great deal of trepidation, to accept nomination, and attended the fateful meeting of the newly elected General Committee in a veritable cold sweat of funk. I voted for myself as instructed, but was greatly relieved to find that it wasn't necessary, as the count showed that I was elected by a comfortable majority. J.R. Jones was made Vice-Chairman. I was promptly installed in the vacant chair and the proceedings of the new committee began.

The first matter to arise was distinctly awkward. W. J. Monk, the Chairman of the Shanghai Club, tendered his resignation. He had only stood for election after considerable persuasion. He now felt that he had deliberately been asked to stand as a sure vote catcher, in order to push Harry Arnhold off the committee. A gentleman if ever there was one, nothing would now persuade him to stay. No course was left but to accept his resignation, and in due course, H.E. Arnhold was co-opted back onto the committee. We felt that we could not afford to be without his vast experience.

To say that I was kept busy from then on would be putting it mildly. The B.R.A. work expanded enormously as the community buckled down to the task of making the maximum possible contribution to the war effort.

Numerous special sub-committees had been set up to deal with the Association's work, and I was an ex-officio member of them all. The increasingly tense political situation added growing importance to the regular reports sent home to Mr O.M. Green, our very able Parliamentary contact in London.

One of the more interesting jobs in which I was engaged was on an investigatory committee set up by the Commercial Secretary to the Embassy, Mr. J.C. Hutchison, for the purpose of investigating enemy trading activity. Germany was straining every nerve to bring in much needed cargoes from all sources remaining open to her. Our job on this committee was to help 'Hutch' keep track of cargoes moving to Germany via the Trans-Siberian Railway, and to devise means of preventing these materials from falling into the hands of the Germans or of their agents. The ways and means employed to overcome this were many and devious. We had not spent our years in the East without, perhaps unconsciously, acquiring a certain amount of oriental cunning ourselves.

Another very interesting job, on account of its curious international character, was a price control committee which I set up at the request of the Municipal Council. At that time, the serious shortage of supplies of imported goods was making itself felt, and profiteering by Chinese retailers was rife. This would normally have been a matter for action by the SMC itself, but the delicacy of the political situation, with Japanese and puppet Chinese on the Council, made it preferable to attempt to handle it through unofficial sources. My own task was not without international complications. The Germans had for many years been the largest suppliers of pharmaceuticals to China, and they still had very large stocks indeed. Without their co-operation, any scheme would prove useless.

The scheme was the essence of simplicity. All importers handling any of the products concerned would be asked to join an association for the control of retail prices, and would pledge themselves to support it. They would individually fix retail prices for their goods, which would be circulated to all retailers and advertized to the public. If any retailer sold a product of any member of the association at above the fixed price, then all members of the association would refuse to supply the retailer with anything that they handled. A scheme of this kind would not work under normal competitive conditions, but with practically everything in short supply, and likely to remain so for an indefinite period, importers could pick and choose their markets without fear of losing business.

The crux of the problem was whether or not the Germans would play.

If it sounds a little queer that we should contemplate working with our enemies, it must be remembered that we were working for the International Settlement in which we all lived, and that it was therefore not so peculiar from our point of view, that we did not allow international differences elsewhere to affect our course of action in this unique stamping ground. I sent out circulars inviting all importers to attend a preliminary meeting. The Germans turned up with the rest and to my great relief, announced their intention of working with us for the common good. Having got the association well under way I turned it over to John M. Hykes. Pearl Harbor supervened before long, but the arrangements worked long enough to prove that it was a practicable solution to the problem.

On Saturdays and Sundays since the outbreak of war I had been section leader of one of the Anti-Sabotage Squads. This had been organized in order to provide additional guards for all Allied Shipping using the port. Continuous day and night watch was maintained by these Volunteer Guards. Taking it all round I did not find time hung heavily on my hands.

It was apparent during 1941 that affairs in the Pacific were working up to a climax. All employees who could be spared were sent away. All those men who could afford to do so and whose wives were amenable to persuasion, were sending their families to places which, it was hoped, would be safer than Shanghai.

I could not persuade my own wife to leave until 1 December 1941. We had been driven from our home, either jointly or separately, by stress of wars of one kind or another far too often, and we had sworn that each time would be the last. On adding it up I could remember eight distinct occasions. The last one was 1937 when some six or seven thousand Chinese and a sprinkling of foreigners were killed and wounded on 14 August by the explosion of four Chinese aerial bombs intended for the *Idzumo*, the Japanese flagship in Chinese waters. On that occasion I had sent my wife and two children to Hong Kong together with all the women and children for whom accommodation could be found.

Hong Kong is pretty unbearable in mid-summer at the best of times. Under these conditions it must have been a little hell and I was not surprised when I had a cable from Japan a few weeks later to say that my family was on its way back. I was not clear as to why the cable should come from Japan, but that soon explained itself. Hong Kong was still not allowing evacuated families to return to Shanghai but was only too glad to see them go elsewhere to relieve congestion. Bunty, being rapid on the uptake, hopped on an 'Empress' boat to Japan and then trans-shipped to a French liner bound for Shanghai.

Her experience as an evacuee on this occasion made her very reluctant indeed to face the prospect again, but a compromise was finally reached. This was that she should go to Java and remain there for a bit. If things blew over, I would take an early summer holiday and fetch her back. If the worst happened she could get from there to the States or to Canada. So I finally saw them off on a Dutch ship, the *Tjisadane*. They sailed together with Marjorie Rose and daughter Anne, whose father Murray was going to live with me. It was hard to see them go, because I had very little hope of that holiday in Java for the coming summer, and God alone knew how many years the war would last if it came, or whether I should see the end of it.

December 1941 was a fateful month. The next farewell I had to make was to the British Marines. This I did in a speech made after a lunch given for Colonel Howard and the officers of the Fourth Marines. They had been stationed in Shanghai since 1937 and had become very popular with the British Community, particularly for their sporting activities. They had taken up Rugger with a will, and their many struggles in which their youth, fitness and speed were matched against the Shanghai team would not readily be forgotten. They ended up by winning and from that day on their place in our hearts was secure. A few short weeks after they left Shanghai they were in action against the Japanese in the Philippines, and were still fighting when Corregidor finally fell. I shall never forget asking Colonel Howard, next to whom I was sitting at this farewell lunch, what he thought of the prospects of war with Japan.

'It is not a question of whether, but when', was his answer.

The British troops had already left, but this was understandable in view of commitments in Europe. With the departure of the Marines we felt defenceless and bare. We had only a few days to go before the balloon went up and put an end to our major uncertainties.

3
PEARL HARBOR

6.15 on the morning of 8 December 1941. I am sound asleep when the extension telephone at my bedside rings:

'Duggie here. It has started. The Japanese have just bombed Pearl Harbor.'

'What the . . . Are you sure? How do you know?'

'I'm at the Race Course, and the news has just come through; and they sank the *Peterel* last night.'*

'But I didn't hear anything', hoping that my failure to hear would make it untrue.

'It's true all right. I thought I had better let you know right away.'

So that was that. Five minutes later the Boy appeared and handed me a leaflet which he said had been dropped in the garden by a Japanese plane. I hadn't heard that either, but it proved that things could really happen without my knowing about them.

The leaflet announced the Declaration of War by His Imperial Japanese Majesty on the United States of America and Great Britain. It stated that for our protection the Japanese Army would enter the Settlement at 10 a.m. sharp, and instructed us to pursue our normal avocations. Warnings were issued against the creation of disorder.

Breakfast was a hurried affair whilst arrangements were made for some of us to go to the office by car whilst others remained in the Crescent, our staff compound, to do what could be done to protect the women in the event of any disorder. The radio had not been able to do more than confirm the bare news of the bombing of Pearl Harbor. It repeated the Japanese proclamation endlessly.

---

* HMS *Peterel*, a small river gunboat, and the USS *Wake*, a ship of approximately the same size, were the sole remaining representatives of allied naval might in Shanghai by December 1941. They had been left moored in the Whangpoo River off the Shanghai Bund principally to enable the embassies to maintain direct radio communication with their capitals.

My worries were not lessened by thoughts of my wife and family, barely a week at sea. Where were they now? Probably somewhere between Hong Kong and Manila, in seas which had been controlled by the Japanese Navy for months past. It was a very long time before I heard the full tale of their adventure.

Four of our Directors, Haley, Gillespie, Farmer, and Cook were away, leaving the conduct of company affairs to Jackson and myself. Too few for the job that this might be. Two cars set off for the office, I drove the leading car. We thought it better to leave the Chinese chauffeurs behind. I don't know what we expected; I know that I breathed a sigh of relief as each intersection was safely passed, and no Japanese troops appeared. Most shops were shut, and there were few pedestrians, but the tension was something that could be felt. The office was reached without incident, and we scattered to our allotted tasks.

These had been worked out in detail for many months past. Every man throughout the organization knew exactly what had to be done. We had in fact already started. It had always appeared to us possible that advance information of an impending crisis might be picked up in Hong Kong before it was known in Shanghai. We had asked Gillespie in Hong Kong to keep us informed if he could. Two days earlier he had cabled the words:

'THE TIME HAS COME.'

How he knew I don't yet know, but it was enough to get us started on our 'emergency measures'. Cash in US dollars and local notes had already been salted away. All documents had been carefully sorted and classified and all those whose possession might prove dangerous or which might give useful information to the enemy had been stacked together in readiness for destruction.

Ours was probably one of the first fires to get started that morning, but it was not long before we were joined by many others. We did not know how soon it would be before the Japanese would walk into the office, and we did not want to be caught with incriminating documents in our possession. We had among other things a very fine and probably unique set of maps, prepared through the course of years of travel by our agricultural and general sales staff. Letters, reports, accounts, code books, everything went into the maw of the furnace; all except one set of private code books. This had been kept at home by Katz, our confidential stenographer, to deal with urgent cables arriving at night or over weekends. He lived in a centrally heated flat with no fireplace. The code books, two large octavo volumes of some hundred pages each, were printed on very heavy and durable paper. The Katz family promptly sat down, reduced the books to scrap paper and flushed them down the toilet. How many hundreds of times they must have pulled that trigger I cannot imagine, but the contemplation of this family conclave gave us many a laugh when we got round to seeing the humorous side of things again.

We had been too busy during the morning even to look out of the windows. We had received reports that the Japanese forces entered the Settlement as specified at 10 a.m., were patrolling the streets, and that this had apparently gone off without incident. The sight that met our eyes on stepping into the street was almost unbelievable. The air was thick with paper ash, and the ground was already almost completely hidden under a carpet of ash. Every office was burning, burning as hard as they could, every scrap of paper that they felt it necessary to destroy. This went on for days, and it is surprising that the Japanese took no steps to stop it. The banks could not do much as they were entered and taken over that day, but it was some weeks before the Japanese got round to sealing off all the larger business premises. Some of the smaller ones were never touched until they were closed by the internment of their personnel.

I had lunch at the Shanghai Club, and saw there some members of the committee of the American Association. We discussed the situation with particular reference to the possibility of continuing the work of the national associations. With the internment of the Embassy and Consular staffs it was obvious that our communities would need to have somebody to turn to for help and to represent their interests vis-à-vis the Japanese. It was clear to me that no such body could function adequately unless it were recognized by the Japanese. Our functions would have to be, ostensibly at least, entirely non-political, and we should have to dress the organizations up in some form which would be likely to obtain their approval.

I also saw W.J. Monk at the Club, and obtained from him a first-hand account of the sinking of HMS *Peterel*. His bedroom at the Club overlooked the river where the *Peterel* was moored, and he had been awakened by the crash of artillery fire from a battery drawn up on the Bund opposite the *Peterel*, and from a destroyer moored about a thousand yards down-stream. The *Peterel* did not have time to fire a shot, and within twenty minutes her crew were swimming for the shore, and the ship herself, a flaming wreck, was sinking beneath the muddy waters of the Whangpoo. One man, A.B. Linkhorn, was killed and several were wounded. All the survivors were picked up, mostly by Chinese sampans, taken prisoner by the Japanese, and finally incarcerated in the camp set up at Woosung for the prisoners of war.

Representatives of the British and American Associations held a meeting during the afternoon, and we decided that we should try to establish contact with the appropriate Japanese authorities. We would ask that the Associations be allowed to set up organizations for the relief of the distress which was bound to ensue, and we should offer to act as intermediaries between them and our communities. We realized that any action on these lines might lay us open to the charge of collaboration, but knowing something of Japanese methods we felt it to be most desirable that we should do everything we could to obviate the necessity for any direct contact between Japanese officialdom and the individual members of our community. We felt that once we had been able to obtain official recognition of our relief organizations, we might be able to do much more than simple relief, as proved to be the case.

Although it was obviously desirable that this line of action should be taken, I was very unhappy at the part which I personally should have to play. I knew how the Japanese liked in these circumstances to have two or three people at the top on whom they could put the finger if things did not go just as they liked. I took a very dim view of the prospect of being one of those on whom the said finger would be likely to fall. I made a few half-hearted attempts to suggest that the Association would do better to select someone with more experience than myself for the job, but my committee were unanimous in disclaiming any desire for the honour. I don't blame them.

We decided to make enquiries through one Okazaki, a Japanese member of the Municipal Council, and to obtain his advice, and if possible his introduction, as to the appropriate official to whom proposals should be submitted. Word came through in due course that we could contact Lt. Kawai of the Japanese Gendarmerie, who had charge of Gendarmerie activities in the area. We felt the fact of our being referred to the Gendarmerie was distinctly ominous. We well knew that they were not nice people, just how lacking in nicety many of us were to learn by bitter experience.

Thus, the morning of 11 December found Anderson, of the American Association, and myself calling on Lt. Kawai at Gendarmerie Headquarters in Hamilton House, in company with one of the Japanese secretaries of the Shanghai Municipal Council. We were to find that Kawai did not need an interpreter but like nearly all Japanese officials he invariably used one. They appeared to find it beneath their dignity to speak such a barbarous tongue as English.

Kawai was a particularly saturnine looking individual with the 'Gendarme look' which we were to come to know so well. We explained the purpose of our call, stressing the relief angle, and the assistance which such an organization might offer to them in ensuring that their instructions were properly understood, and in clearing up possible misunderstandings. We had not gone very far before he suggested, as we feared he would, that he would be glad to accept our offer to be responsible for the good behaviour, and submission to Japanese instructions, of our communities. We had, of course, to disclaim our ability to do this although we were prepared to urge compliance with all reasonable instructions, and we were particularly anxious to avoid all undesirable incidents. Each side knew perfectly well what the other was aiming at. Anderson and I fully realized that we could not hope to avoid a large measure of personal responsibility for the actions and attitudes of our respective communities, but we were definitely not prepared to admit it. We also had to tread very delicately in this our first official contact with the conqueror, until we learned just how far we could safely go in pressing our arguments.

Kawai finally said that he thought that permission would probably be granted, but that he would have to refer the matter to a higher authority. Anderson and I then took our leave, and not ill pleased with the progress that we had made, repaired to the Shanghai Club for a much needed bracer and lunch.

We were half-way through our meal when we heard muffled sounds of disturbance from below. A few minutes later Ward, the Club Secretary, entered the dining room accompanied by a Japanese Naval Officer and two ratings, armed to the teeth. Ward called for silence and announced in a very agitated voice that the Japanese had come to take over the Club, and that the whole premises must be completely vacated in twenty minutes. No one would be permitted to carry anything with him. The officer clanked out followed by Ward, and the ratings remained on guard at the door.

Three or four members who lived in the Club left immediately for their rooms to see if they could save anything of their personal belongings, the remainder continued their meal, and apart from a certain heightening in the level of conversation no one would have realized that the members were about to be submitted to the indignity of being turned out neck and crop from these sacrosanct premises. I remained to finish my meal with the others but the food had most definitely lost its savour.

The American Club was taken over by the Navy in a similar way at about the same time. They not only took over the premises of both Clubs, but also the pavements outside them. Pedestrians wishing to pass them had either to walk in the roadway or to cross to the other side of the street. They were also required to raise hats and bow to the 'poached eggs' fluttering in the doorway. This must have been a sad blow to the hat section of the outfitting trade, because it did not take many days of this for people to realize the advantages gained by going hatless.

On the following day, Anderson and I received instructions from the Gendarmerie that we should call at Naval Headquarters in Hongkew and see Lt. Commander Ohtani. At this interview we were told that our request to be allowed to set up relief organizations had been approved and that they would be under the joint surveillance of the Navy, and the Gendarmerie, both of whom would appoint a supervisor to keep tabs on our activities. All inward and outward correspondence must be seen and approved by supervisors, and no action must be taken without their knowledge. We must submit a complete list of our committee, and of all employees or volunteer staff.

Our first request was that they should help us to find offices. The B.R.A., together with the British Chamber of Commerce, had used that part of the top floor of the Jardine building which was not used by the British Embassy, and when the Embassy premises had been sealed, our office had been sealed at the same time. I was not particularly anxious to draw attention to this slight error, as owing to a slip up, none of the B.R.A. papers had been destroyed and there were a number of compromising reports to London over my signature which I thought they would find definitely displeasing. The American Association had also lost their offices with the taking over of the American Club, so both Associations were homeless. They finally established both Associations in the offices of the American President Line, where the photographs of Robert Dollar and his sons looked down on us from the panelled walls. In the meantime I had started work.

4

REGISTRATION AND SUPERVISION

In January 1942, the Japanese promulgated the first regulation affecting the enemy communities. All enemy residents must produce photographs and passports and attend an office on the Bund within three days, for the purposes of registration. Thereafter, any enemy national found on the streets without his or her registration card would be liable to summary punishment.

The registration offices were small, and the staff hopelessly inadequate. It was clear from the outset that they could not possibly complete the job in the allotted three days or anything like it. Trouble started immediately. Over-zealous sentries started demanding registration cards right away, and I had to see officials at the registration office to try to get the matter adjusted. Next, they would not give cards to the many people whose passports were out of date. Worse still, there were many others who, having been born in Shanghai and having never had occasion to leave it, had no passports at all. The Swiss Consulate had just announced that they had been appointed by the British Government to take charge of the interests of British nationals. Their instructions from the British Embassy were very explicit and unfortunately did not permit them to issue, extend, or amend passports in any manner whatsoever. Apparently this is a very jealously guarded privilege.

I returned again to the registration office, fought my way through the massed crowd of applicants waiting ouside closed doors, and found the harassed officials making a meal of Japanese cakes and tea. They were polite but firm, passports must be up to date. There was no moving them on this. They were civil servants, brought up in the best traditions of red tape, and regulations were made to be obeyed, not adapted to circumstances.

I then had to go into the question of those who had no passports. The arguments were endless, but I thought I saw a loophole. If the regulations said thus and thus, then it must be so, appearances must be maintained, face must be saved. I tore back to the office, got hold of a passport and sent the faithful and invaluable 'Jumbo', my office secretary, to the Chinese stationer who supplied our company requirements, with instructions to do a rush job on making me rubber stamps duplicating faithfully all the Consular stamps in the passport. The only difference was to be that instead of the magic words 'His Britannic Majesty's Consulate General ... Consul', should appear the words 'British Residents' Association of China ... Chairman'.

The job was faithfully done in a few hours, and the rubber stamps were on my makeshift desk, ready for the experiment. The anxious but willing victims of the experiment were also there, out of date passports in hand, eager to try anything which might afford a way out of the impasse and get them the much needed registration card.

I knew it would take several hours for these people to work their way to the head of the queue and to present their passports with the fake extensions to the registration officials. It was no use going on with it until I heard whether or not they would pass muster. In the meantime there was the question of the unfortunate without passports. I was not prepared to risk anything with them until I knew how the less difficult job was succeeding, but in the meantime preparations could be made.

Few of these people were known personally to me, or to any of the small band of helpers whom I had time to gather together. What I was proposing to do was to give them some form of passport as a British citizen. In doing that I was going to recognize them as members of the community for which the Japanese were going to make me responsible. I could not afford to take unnecessary chances on making mistakes over this. My first step therefore was to interview these people, and tell them that they must bring me proofs of identity and letters of reference from employers or from substantial British citizens. Some of them were inclined to protest at this. They were overwrought, but so was I.

I insisted on dictating my terms because I was taking the bigger risk. I was prepared to take my chance of several hundred years' imprisonment by the British Government for making unauthorized entries in British passports, but I wasn't going to risk admitting to the fold some undesirables of unknown antecedents for whose actions the Japanese might hold me responsible. After all, the Japanese were a great deal nearer and infinitely more menacing than the British Government.

Late that afternoon, the first of my B.R.A. extensions began to trickle back, grateful and triumphant. The chops had worked and they had got their registration cards. The case of those without passports was somewhat more difficult. I had no blank passports, and it was not practicable to have imitations made. I compromised by issuing certificates of identity and recognition of status as a British subject in lieu of a passport. These had photographs, stamps and signatures all over them. After a little initial difficulty, they also did the trick.

Two days later we were installed in the President Line offices and met our Japanese supervisors. One proved to be a friend of Kaneda, the chief Japanese salesman in our office. I recollected having seen him in the office several times in the past year, and I wondered then, not without apprehension, whether his visits had had some motive other than his desire to chat with his friend.

The other supervisor, appointed by the Navy, was a young civilian business man named Kira. He had, I think, no connection with the Navy, and had probably been chosen for his knowledge of English which was quite fair. He was a complete contrast to the Gendarmerie representative. He was small and slim, one of the tiniest male Japanese I have ever seen, with a long oval face that looked effeminate. There must have been much more male in him than was apparent, because a few months later he acquired much face in the eyes of his Japanese friends by becoming the father of twin boys, a particularly rare phenomenon among the heavenly race. He tried to be stern and dominating as befitted the chosen representative of conquering Nippon, but he simply could not hold the pose. We soon found that he could be handled and we arrived at a tacit arrangement whereby we submitted only a token selection of correspondence for his approval. After all, he knew perfectly well that we were not going to put anything compromising into writing, and our activities were, on the surface at least, very humdrum and innocuous. This also gave him lots of time for his private business affairs, and his favourite sport — playing the slot machines at Jimmy's Kitchen.

The Executive Committee of the B.R.A. started to meet daily. At first, chairs were placed for our two Japanese watchdogs, and we tried to explain our discussions to them as we went along. These were chiefly concerned with the organization of relief and means of raising funds — the legal ones of course, and our mentors were not long in losing interest. We put our conference table right next to Kira's desk so that he could sit in his swivel chair and listen to us over his shoulder. Finally, we virtually ignored him, and after the meetings I submitted a brief and well edited note of our discussions to him. This was most satisfactory. What greater proof of his zeal could he show than to produce for his superiors a written report based on the very best of evidence. Kira got away with this for many months, to our great pleasure and relief, but in the end, he went a little too far in the neglect of his duties, and was replaced.

5

THE *PETEREL* SAILORS

A FEW days after the Japanese Navy had installed us in our new offices, I received a message from Commander Ohtani to call on him at the Naval Headquarters. I was specifically instructed that the presence of Anderson, President of the American Association, who had accompanied me on an earlier visit was not required. I thought this a little strange as the Associations were working so closely together. I could think of no reason why I should be required alone. I went as instructed and was ushered into a very pleasant if somewhat garishly furnished room. There were comfortable, if low, divans and chairs, presumably sawn off to Japanese size; an even lower occasional table with a maroon silk cover where reposed cut glass boxes of cigarettes, cigars, and a very inviting looking bottle and glasses. I was just wondering if this was the modern version of the fatted calf when Ohtani entered in full fig, complete with sword. Bows, but fortunately no handshakes to be proffered and ignored.

'Ah, Mr Collar, so pleased to see you. Please be seated. A cigarette? You are no doubt wondering why I have requested you to call at Naval Headquarters this morning.'

'Why, yes.' The only thing that I could think of having done so far that might mean trouble was the little matter of the passports.

Ohtani rose to his feet. I thought I had better do the same. Politeness usually costs nothing.

'Mr Collar, I wish to express to you, as representing the British community in Shanghai, the prrr-ofound admiration of His Imperial Japanese Majesty's Navy for the heroic conduct of Lt. Polkinghorn and the crew of His Majesty's ship *Peterel*, in refusing to surrender when called upon to do so, and in deciding to keep flag flying and to go down with ship. Their conduct is in keeping with the very highest tradition of the British Navy. Japanese Navy so pleased. Also very glad to inform you that no man killed [this was a lie], Lt. Polkinghorn slight wound in hand. One other man little wounded. I ask you to drink with me to health of Lt. Polkinghorn and crew of HMS *Peterel*.'

I was not much in favour of drinking with the Japanese on principle, but this was obviously an occasion. I was really very much touched. I thought that it showed quite unusual generosity of feeling on the part of a Japanese, although we had always felt that their Navy was a distinct cut above their other Services. I was very glad to drink a toast with him and expressed my appreciation of his attitude.

Ohtani then explained that as Aide to the Admiral it had fallen to him personally to board the *Peterel* to demand its surrender and he went on to give me a first hand account of the proceedings. He was much impressed by the formal correctitude of his reception and by the coolness with which Lt. Polkinghorn had received the information of the declaration of war and had made his decision to sink rather than surrender. He repeated several times:

'Polkinghorn very correct, very correct man, very brave man, I think.'

When his recital had finished, I thanked Ohtani for his courtesy in giving me the account, which would naturally be of interest to the whole British community. I also took the opportunity of thanking him for his assistance in finding offices for the Association's relief organization and for enabling us to get this work started. Then I rose to go, feeling that I had taken up enough of his time, and that I myself had plenty of other things to do.

'One moment, Mr. Collar. Not to go yet. One other small matter I wish to discuss.' What was coming now? Somehow that did not sound so good.

'HMS *Peterel* have crew of twenty-seven men. We find list in British Embassy. We only capture twenty-four. I find three men on shore leave on night of 8 December. We make enquiries. We know these men still in Shanghai. We believe they are being hidden. They must surrender themselves. You give them order.'

That fairly took my breath away. So this was the fly in the ointment. I lost no time in protesting that I had no knowledge whatsoever of these men, and that I did not even know if he was correct in saying that there were members of the crew at large. This brought a very sharp rejoinder. The Japanese Navy did not make mistakes of this kind. The facts were as stated and I should be ill-advised to express doubts as to the veracity of a Japanese officer.

Wrong tack, try again. 'Even if the information is correct, I am a mere civilian, without even any authority over the civilian population, let alone a Serviceman. These are members of the British Armed Forces, as such, it is their duty to try to escape, and I have neither the authority nor the desire to instruct them otherwise. In any case, I don't know where they are and have no idea of how to get into contact with them.'

'Mr Collar, Consul-General George now interned by Japanese. You are now in his place.' That was a new thought to me. It put the finger on with a vengeance.

'Consul-General has authority to give order to armed forces in China. You can give order. If British people sheltering these men, you must know all about it. You must order them to surrender immediately. If they surrender themselves now, they will be honourably treated by Japanese Navy. If they not, many searches will be made, every British home will be searched, maybe very unfortunate incidents.'

This with a very meaning inflection.

'Moreover, Japanese Gendarmerie will help Navy men to make search. When catch Gendarmerie will keep. Maybe Gendarmes will not treat so good as Japanese Navy. You must do.'

This was really putting me on the spot. The underlying threat about the possibility of incidents was all too obvious, and too real to be ignored. There was moreover much truth in his suggestion that if they were caught by the Gendarmes they were liable to have a very rough passage, and I was definitely inclined to believe him when he said that if they surrendered to the Navy, they would be received with the honour of war. This was in the early days of the war when Japanese victories were putting them in a relatively good humour and I believed that he had been at least partly sincere in expressing his admiration for the action of the *Peterel*.

On the other hand there was the incontrovertible fact that I didn't know anything about these men, did not know how to set about getting into touch with them, and even if I did, I had no authority whatsoever to give them an order even if I wished to do so. I wanted to avoid trouble for the community, but surely it was my duty to help these men to get away rather than to assist them politely to prison. And here was this indescribable little Japanese telling me that I had to do this revolting deed, or else.

Ohtani then tried a little dirt. 'If you do not wish to order them to surrender, all you have to do is to give me a piece of paper with their address on it. I will attend to the rest.'

That really did annoy me, and I replied that such action was out of the question and the only thing with which I was concerned was whether I had the authority, and if so, whether I should be justified in using it. Whatever was decided would be done openly and above board. He did not repeat the suggestion or make any further reference to it.

I could not think of any new arguments and could only repeat the same ones over in pretty much the same words. Ohtani's retorts were becoming more brief and bitter and finally he lost all patience and said:

'I order you to do this.'

I thought he was going to hit me when I replied that under the circumstances I could not accept the order. I felt that I could not take the responsibility of making a decision myself but I proposed to go back and discuss the matter with senior members of the community who were better able to judge than I what our action could and should be. He was aware that I was inexperienced in public affairs and no action that I took would be effective unless supported by my senior advisers. I was to find that this emphasis on my inexperience, which they knew to be true, was to be helpful in one or two other tight corners.

Although Ohtani did not let up in his attitude, he realized that he could not get any further with me. He finally agreed to allow me to leave, with instructions to come back in twenty-four hours and report what action I had taken. I had not committed myself, as he fully realized, but he also had maintained his position. He was not going to recognize that there was the remotest possibility of his orders not being promptly obeyed. There was no formal leave taking this time. Ohtani turned his back and walked out of the room with a final bark:

'Be here tomorrow.'

I gathered the committee together as soon as I could that afternoon. They were as worried as I was. The Japanese could undoubtedly make things really tough for the whole community if they suspected that these men were being sheltered, and was it right to risk the welfare of six thousand odd men, women and children, against that of these three men? Ohtani probably disbelieved me when I told him that I had no knowledge of the men and no means of making contact with them. Such a thing could not happen in the Japanese community in which the residents' union had real political power and a very comprehensive spy system.

It was agreed that before seeing Ohtani on the morrow I should see the Swiss Consul-General, Mr Emil Fontanel, or his principal assistant, Dr Schilling, to ascertain their views and that we should all make enquiries to see if we could establish contact with the missing men. They both agreed that the course we proposed to take was the proper one under the circumstances. I saw Ohtani again, but had J.R. Jones with me to back me up. He was invaluable on occasions like this and did much to sustain my much frayed moral fibre. Ohtani was angry, as was to be expected, but I think we half convinced him that we could do no more. However, he was insistent that we should report progress, and was on my tail for many weeks thereafter.

I was never able to make direct contact with the sailors. The nearest I got to doing so was when I was told that I might get somewhere if I saw John Huxley of the Fire Brigade. He denied knowing anything of them, as was to be expected. However, I gave him the message that I had for them and believe it was duly passed on. If my recollection is correct, I gave him a signed message accepting the responsibility towards HM Government on behalf of any of these three who should decide to give himself up rather than to escape. One man did actually surrender himself through the Swiss Consulate. I was never able to learn what was the final fate of the other two.

As long as I could stall Ohtani, I preferred to know as little as possible. I often found that there is a great deal of truth in the current catchphrase that 'It pays to be ignorant', especially where the knowledge is inclined to be dangerous. Ohtani kept me in a state of nervous agitation for many weeks, but to my great relief his enquiries finally petered out.

6

BRIDGE HOUSE HORROR

A FEW days after Pearl Harbor, about ten British subjects in Shanghai and a number of Americans were arrested by the Japanese Gendarmerie and disappeared from our ken. From then on ensued a slow but remorseless series of arrests of 'enemy nationals' who vanished into the dark portals of Bridge House, North Szechuen Road, the Gendarmerie Headquarters. Victims were taken from all walks of life, without rhyme or reason. When they eventually came out, they were changed and badly shaken men. None of them talked and with cause.

Among the first group were: 'Bill' Gande, a prominent wine importer; Jacks, a local merchant; Eddy Elias, a sharebroker; Brister Clarke, former head of the Indian Section of the Municipal Police; Harold Reynell, exchange broker and President of the St George's Society; Meyers and Forbes of the Chinese Maritime Customs; and A.H. Gordon, a free-lance photographer. J.B. Powell was prominent among the American victims.

The B.R.A. immediately started to register protests, with the Japanese Consulate, SMC officials, the Swiss Consulate, and every avenue that appeared to offer any hopeful means of approach. Everywhere we came up against a blank wall. Every Japanese to whom I or others spoke froze up immediately. The most that any of them would say was that no one who valued his own health and freedom would attempt to mix in any way with the affairs of the Gendarmerie. The Swiss Consul-General was able to see the head of the Gendarmerie for the Shanghai district and also the local Military C.-in-C. The former said that it was nothing, just a routine check up and the men would be released in three or four days, the latter declined to interest himself in the matter.

Jack Liddell, British Chairman of the Municipal Council at the time of Pearl Harbor, made a special appeal to Okazaki, his successor, in the case of Harold Reynell, his brother-in-law. Reynell was released after about eight days. I know of only two cases where the Gendarmerie allowed themselves to be persuaded to release a victim without first subjecting him to the customary lengthy procedure. The release of Reynell was particularly useful since he had learned something of the routine and had been able to make certain contacts among the guards which enabled him, in the utmost secrecy, to organize a service of food parcels to those left inside. The B.R.A. took this over when it became too big for him to manage alone.

It was always a chancy business; we would send down a small daily parcel containing chocolate, some meat sandwiches, a little fruit, a thermos of hot soup, making the food as concentrated as possible. Vitamin concentrates were mixed in, in various ways. We learned later that the prisoners were not allowed to have these parcels in their cells. When the guards were in a good mood, the prisoners were allowed to go into a special room, there they had to wolf the food down as fast as possible, not knowing when they would be kicked back to their cells. Not all of them had this privilege. We never knew exactly how many men were there and we were not allowed to put names on individual parcels. Some men would come to me on their release, and express their gratitude for the tremendous physical and moral help that these small lots of food had afforded them. Others would upbraid me bitterly for having done nothing to help them. I had a stock answer for the latter: 'We are doing everything we possibly can. I expect to be there myself some day and I am not missing any chance of working up a foolproof routine.'

The food parcels were first made up by the Bakerite Co. until their Japanese supervisors stopped it. Later, Mrs Lewis, who ran a school of cookery in Shanghai, took on the job. She often catered for my company parties in happier days. She started off by sending her Chinese employees down to Bridge House with the food. It says much for their loyalty to her that they ventured to set foot in this place of evil. Even so, they were often turned back at the door. So Mrs Lewis started to go herself. She refused to be turned away. If rebuffed she would wait until the sentry was changed, she might wait for two or even three changes, but in the end she would get in and deposit her precious parcels.

'I'm an old woman', she told me. 'They can only kill me once, but as long as I know those poor boys are in there, I'm going to go on trying to feed them.'

She kept this up for months, through the chill of the winter and the heat of the summer, always dressed in the same rusty black, growing older and more tired before my eyes. She refused to let anyone else take over.

'They are getting used to me now. They even let me watch them eat, once. I don't think anyone else could do it now.'

I knew she was right. I believe the Japanese even came to respect her. There was a bad time in the summer of 1942 when there was a complete change of personnel at Bridge House. It took her many weeks to get to terms with the new crowd. They had the effrontery to say that they could not allow food in from outside during the summer owing to the danger of cholera. Their solicitude for their prisoners was such that they could not permit them to eat any food which had not been cooked under their own careful and loving eyes: two bowls of rice a day. It was fortunate that during this particular period when we could get nothing in, the number of prisoners in Bridge House was lower than at any period, but that did not make it any less unhappy for the few.

It was some time before we heard that Gande, Brand, Jacks, Elias, Brister, and several others had been transferred from Bridge House to the military barracks at Kiangwan and that they were being tried for espionage. They were finally sentenced to varying terms of imprisonment which they started serving in the Ward Road Gaol. Here the feeding problem was much easier, and was taken over by their relatives. There were still some British warders in the gaol and they also did everything possible to lessen the rigors of prison life.

In these early days, the treatment of the European prisoners at Bridge House was not as bad as it became later on. There were relatively few cases of questioning under actual torture, which was the rule rather than the exception after the repatriation of the Embassy and Consular officials in the summer of 1942. It was nevertheless quite horrible. The whole process followed a carefully thought out and no doubt tried and proven procedure, designed to break down morale and to reduce resistance to the lowest ebb. This is a rough outline of their *modus operandi* in the later days when they stopped short only at killing their British and American victims. They had no such inhibitions in respect of Chinese and Russian prisoners and those of the minor nations. They would warn our people not to talk, they made sure the others would not.

The arrests were always made at night, around 2 a.m. seemed to be the favourite time. From the point of view of the victim it was the worst possible hour at which to be wakened from a warm bed and confronted with the chill menace of drawn swords and loaded pistols. You would be ordered to dress, but could take nothing with you beyond possibly a packet of cigarettes; out into the night and hustled into a fast car. It was a quick run, through the deserted streets, over the Szechuen Road Bridge and down North Szechuen Road, a sharp turn to the left and there was Bridge House, once a hotel, still open to guests, but definitely shorn of the usual amenities.

The reception office: turn out all pockets, remove tie, braces, suspenders, shoes, anything that you might hang or otherwise damage yourself with. All you can keep in addition to your suit of clothing is one handkerchief, provided that it was not too large — it must not be long enough to go round a neck. You are run down stairs along a corridor, and shoved into a small room, maybe ten by ten containing perhaps twelve, fifteen, twenty shapeless lumps that you assume to be people, huddled together on the floor for warmth. The first thing to hit you is the smell, it is solid, sickening, the fetid stink of filthy unwashed humanity, mingled with the odours of ordure and the faint but unmistakable scent of approaching death. You were not feeling exactly cheerful before getting here, but this simply takes the heart right out of you. It is unbelievable that people can actually live and survive in this appalling hole. Surely they have made a mistake in putting you in here. There can't possibly be room for one more. The guard says 'No talk', slams the door and departs. Room is made for you somehow. You don't recognize anyone you know among these filthy scarecrows with long matted hair and beards, but some of them recognize you. You don't believe it, they simply can't be the men you spoke to in the street or office only a few weeks ago, and you think to yourself, 'God, shall I become like that?'

After whispered greetings and giving them the news of the outside world, you try to sleep. The reaction has left you dead tired, even the hard boards would not keep you awake, but the bugs do.

In the morning, you begin to get sorted out. Your cell mates are of all nationalities, including probably a Japanese whom you suspect of being a stool-pigeon. There are probably one or two women there too, a delicate thought on the part of the Japanese, it makes it so much more awkward for both parties. You see, the toilet is just a hole in the floor, or a bucket in the corner which frequently overflows before it is allowed to be emptied.

No talking is permitted in the cells, no reading or smoking, or any form of pleasurable relaxation of any kind. Except when otherwise ordered you must sit cross-legged on the floor and meditate. Just try it, especially if you are a big man. I saw Hector Forsyth the day he came out. At six feet two, he normally weighed about 200 lbs. He was down to under

130 lbs and the flesh on his buttocks was literally worn away almost to the bone. He had had to sit on a concrete floor for six weeks, day in and day out.

Breakfast is due at 7 a.m. or maybe 8 a.m., it may not come until midday or the guards may forget it altogether. When it comes, it is a small bowl of boiled rice, and a dish of tea, lukewarm to cold. You learn that this may be all you will get to drink today so you had better make it last. You get an evening meal too. Another bowl of rice, this time usually with a small piece of pickled vegetable, or a speck of raw salt fish. This is your daily food.

Twice a day, you all rise together, form a crocodile and do the prison shuffle round the cell, for half an hour if you can stand that long. Washing is variable. Some guards allow prisoners out once daily for a five minute wash under a tap in the yard, others make it once a week. You can do nothing about your clothes, unless as sometimes happens, clean underclothes are allowed to be sent in.

This is your life whilst awaiting your turn, cold, hungry, dirty, vermin ridden. You might have some idea why they picked you up, you might have no idea at all. It makes no difference. You just sit there, waiting, waiting until they come to fetch you. There is no telling how long you will have to wait, seldom less than ten days. Sometimes much more. It might even be many weeks, so long that you feel sure you have been forgotten. But whilst you are waiting, others in your cell have their turn. At night, always at night, the guards would unlock the door and call a name. Hours later he or she would return, perhaps with no more than a bruised and inflamed face, perhaps covered in blood and more dead than alive. How will you return when your turn comes? Will you be able to take it? How the hell can you tell. You have never had to face anything like this. You hear their tales, told in whispers, all the horrid, bloody details. You are still waiting, and whilst you wait, some in your cell die. Others are taken at night and never come back, a fortunate one may be released, but every night you hear the thumps, and shrieks and groans, and wonder, quaking inwardly, how you will take it.

You realize too that all this time you are becoming less and less able to take it. However tough you were physically and morally before you came in, the treatment is sapping your strength, and you know that that is just what it is meant to do. You are being scientifically conditioned for the questioning.

It is almost a relief when your turn comes. Upstairs to a bare room, with a desk, a chair or two, a wooden trestle, some bamboo fencing swords leaning against a corner. A Japanese in plain clothes sits at the desk smoking, another is beside him. Very likely he pulls a gun from a shoulder holster as though it irked him and throws it carelessly on the desk, the butt almost within reach of your hand. You know all about that. The chaps downstairs have warned you about it. The gun is unloaded, and they would just love you to make a grab for it some night when you are at the end of your tether.

The questions begin, routine stuff, name, age, address, names of relatives, friends, education, job, all that the apparently meaningless government questionnaires always have. But there is a difference. These chaps don't seem to believe your answers to even these straightforward questions. At every third or fourth question the interrogator calls you a liar and the assistant gives you a sharp slap across the face. They question you *ad nauseam* on all the routine stuff for two, three hours, and you are finally returned to your cell, still without any inkling of what you are there for.

You will probably wait another ten days before you are taken out again. This time you are stripped stark naked before the questioning starts. It is so much more undignified and it makes you feel more defenceless, as in fact you are. They can get at any particular spot they want to now and no bother. This time they use a stick on your flanks or buttocks if they don't like your answers, one of those bamboo fencing swords probably made out of half a dozen strips of bamboo fitted with a hilt and tied together at the point. They sting and have quite a cutting edge if drawn in at the moment of impact. The questions are getting nearer something now, but you still are not sure what exactly they are trying to find out. This is still part of the conditioning process, so back you go to the cell again exhausted and in considerable pain, perhaps bleeding a bit here and there.

Another wait of several days, more questioning and beating, you are getting pretty low now, and dread the ordeal more and more each time. Each time they are a little harder on you, perhaps you have some cigarette burns here and there now, nothing deliberate of course, one of them happened to be near you when his smoke was finished and you were nearest to stub it on, and then of course they smoke quite a lot.

They are beginning to get hot now, their questions begin to make a pattern. It isn't at all what you thought they might be after you for, but they seem to think you were mixed up in another affair about which you know nothing whatever. You are not sure if this is a good thing or not. Perhaps it is easier to deny knowledge that you haven't got, than to refuse answering a question to which you do know the answer. It is easier in one way of course because you can't tell what you don't know, however severe the torture, but since they are very persistent people the chances are that they will give you all they have got.

No long waits now, meditation does not seem to be doing you any good so you get it night after night. Thumbs are tied together with string behind your back and a rope over a pulley lifts you off the ground with a jerk that nearly dislocates your shoulders, back to the ground with a thump, up again, down again, until you faint with pain. A little bastinado across the soles of your feet. The electric bath, this is really intriguing. One terminal of an electric circuit goes into the water in which you are standing or sitting, the other is touched delicately to various parts of your anatomy. None of this makes you remember what you don't know, so next comes the *pièce de résistance*, the water cure. You are spread-eagled over a wooden stool, hands and feet tied down to its legs. Water is poured into your mouth until you go through all the sensations of drowning and you lose consciousness. You come round finally and they ask you again, same answer, same treatment, same answer. You wish to hell you did know something to tell them, anything to stop this unbelieveable pain. As a last resort they fill you up once again, and when all the body cavities are full, one of them jumps on your stomach. The water gets out where it can, straining and tearing your insides. After the first searing pain you don't feel anything more for a bit, you are out cold, but the coming round is pretty terrible too.

That is about as far as they will go unless they are prepared to finish you off altogether. After that you are asked to sign a confession, in Japanese. You probably do it, you would sign anything now, and you know that this means that they have finished with you. You have had more than three months of it and they seldom take more than one hundred days. You are probably moved to a different cell now and given slightly more food, not much, but a little extra means a great deal to you. Finally the day comes when you are taken upstairs for the last time. You are not sure of it until you get there and they tell you that you are going to be set free. Just a few formalities first: a paper to sign saying that you have been well treated and that you will not divulge to anybody any information whatsoever regarding the happenings of the past hundred days. This is accompanied by a grim warning:

'If you talk, you come back.'

You don't talk.

7

THREATS AND UNCERTAINTY

ONE night about two months after the Japanese attack on Pearl Harbor, I was out at the Swiss Consulate General in Avenue Joffre and was talking to M. Kobelt when his phone rang.

'It's the Gendarmerie, they want to speak to you.' My heart dropped into my boots. What on earth could they want with me at this time of night? I took the phone very gingerly. It was Sato, the legal adviser to the Gendarmerie who had first been assigned to keep an eye on us in the B.R.A. office.

'Have very important secret job for you. One English man very sick, I hand him over to you, I want you to go to Bridge House to fetch him.'

'What's that? I don't quite understand.'

Message repeated.

'When do I go, right now? Can he walk or shall I need an ambulance? Have the guards received their instructions? Could you come with me to make sure that there is no difficulty?'

'Ah yes, maybe trouble. First you come to my room, Metropole Hotel, be here six thirty while I arrange everything.'

I didn't like this at all. It was something quite new. It might be genuine, but on the other hand it might just be a means of getting me to walk into Bridge House without fuss or bother. This would be a job for J.R. Jones if only I were lucky enough to find him at this time of night, but first, what about transport. I had no car now, and had come to the Consulate on my bicycle. It was five miles to Bridge House from here and I couldn't fetch a sick man on a bicycle anyway. I asked Kobelt if there was a chance of borrowing a consular car. The only one available was Fontanel's personal car which was offered without a moment's hesitation. I had an appointment with Fontanel the following morning and I arranged that if I should not turn up, they would start to make a fuss, not that I expected it to do any good. I also arranged with them to get hold of Dr Gauntlett, to warn him that he might be needed, and ask him to arrange to have a room ready at the Country Hospital.

J.R. was fortunately at home, and I picked him up in the car before going to the Metropole. He agreed that it might just be a ruse to get hold of me, in which case he would know right away and would do what was possible. I told him what jobs were outstanding on my desk in case I didn't get back.

We arrived at the Metropole and made our way to Sato's room. My personal anxieties were quickly relieved when he said that there was no objection to J.R. Jones going with me in case I needed help and he explained that I was to fetch 'Mr Crark' who was very sick. But first I must sign a little paper.

Sato leaned forward to his desk and opened a drawer, pulled out first a loaded automatic, secondly a sheet of paper. These were placed on the desk top, side by side. Typical Gendarmerie stuff. He then started to compose a suitable document, finally producing a statement to the effect that Mr G.E. Clarke was being released into my personal care and that I must undertake to produce him whenever called upon to do so by the Gendarmerie. I must further undertake to give no information whatsoever to other people as to Mr Clarke's condition and to divulge no information as to what I might see or hear whilst in Bridge House. Both Jones and I signed this and Sato added:

'Must promise very strictly not to talk of what you see. Gendarmerie very strict about this. If you no obey perhaps you go to Bridge House, stay there, I think you do not like that.'

I explained that if Clarke was very ill he would have to accept a doctor and hospital attendants knowing of Clarke's condition.

'All right, you must tell them no talk. You are responsible.'

It was an impossible condition, but if the Gendarmerie were letting Clarke go he must be very ill indeed and this was no time to quibble over details.

Sato gave us a card of introduction to Sergeant-Major Yamamoto in charge of Bridge House, and phoned him before we left, to tell him that we were on our way. You will note that the senior officer was only a sergeant-major. Rank did not mean much in the Gendarmerie. Kawai, in charge of the Settlement and Concession areas, was only a first lieutenant, and later, in Haiphong Road camp, the highest ranking Gendarme we had was a corporal who appeared to be in a position to give orders to the army colonel.

Neither Jones nor I knew exactly where the entrance to Bridge House was to be found and we had quite a hunt for it. There were no loiterers in that neighbourhood from whom enquiries might be made. We found it in the end and went into a gloomy, ill lit guardroom where we were received by a surly second class private at the desk. I asked for the sergeant-major and showed Sato's card. It seemed to me that there were meaning grins and sniggers from some of the lounging guard. It was evident that we were not regarded as persons to whom any form of respect was due although I gathered that they were not accustomed to see foreigners walk into the place without an escort.

We were taken up an outside stairway of the inner courtyard to an office on the second floor. It was simply crammed with desks at each of which clerks were busily writing. The S.M. did not waste much time on us. He was a slight man in civvies and did not look particularly sinister.

'You have seen Mr Sato. You know what you have to do. You have signed paper. Remember, you must not talk. First please sign receipt.'

I signed.

'There Mr Clarke. You take away.' I turned round. 'Where?' Surely not that, I thought. That can't possibly be Clarke.

'Come on,' said Jones, 'that's him.'

'How are you old man?' A conventional greeting if ever the word meant anything.

A dirty unkempt, cringing creature, with long matted hair and beard falling over the staring whiteness of a new bandage round head and throat was crouching down between two guards who had just thrust him into the room. Jones took hold of him immediately and started to walk out. The sergeant-major held me back.

'Where you take him?'

'Country Hospital, he looks very ill.'

'Yes, maybe die. You report to me every day. Maybe if get better, I must take back.'

I resolved immediately that if he didn't die, it was going to take him a hell of a long time to get better, and that with Gauntlett's backing, we would keep him hovering between life and death for as long as we humanly could.

I hurried after Jones and caught him up just before they reached the car. Clarke had not yet said anything intelligible and we weren't wasting time on talk. We got in the back with Clarke between us. It took quite an effort to do so, not because he was so weak, but because of the smell, sickly, nauseating. Then we started to tell him that he was all right now, we were taking him away.

'And I shan't have to go back?'

'No — you are out now and we are taking you to the Country Hospital. We will bath you and put you to bed and then bring your wife to see you.'

'Thank God, thank God, the wonderful fresh air. Free. I never thought I would see it again.'

He was shivering and I took off my scarf and coat and wrapped them round him, not entirely without reluctance. I should have to clean and debug them before wearing them again, a petty thought under the circumstances.

Gauntlett, stout fellow, was waiting at the hospital and together we took Clarke upstairs to his room. I explained the situation rapidly to Gauntlett, the need for avoidance of chatter, better keep out all visitors except his wife for a bit, try to keep at most two nurses on the job. The order to make a daily report on his condition and my suggestion that the reports should be made as grave as possible was duly noted. Gauntlett had had no time to do more than take a quick look at Clarke and test his pulse, but this was enough to enable him to say that the grave reports would in all honesty not be difficult. I went downstairs to the Reception Office to fill in the necessary admission forms.

I was half-way through this when a car drew up at the door with a scream of tyres on the tarmac and out climbed three Japanese in plain clothes. They pushed through the door and after a moment of uncertainty clattered across to the Reception Desk. I knew them immediately for what they were — Gendarmes.

'Where is Mr Clarke? We want him.'

The girl was bewildered and it was obviously my cue. I explained that I had just brought him in to the hospital on the instructions and with the approval of Mr Sato and Sergeant-Major Yamamato and that I had personally accepted responsibility for him. What did they want with him now? They explained that the Gendarmerie had changed their minds. They were afraid that Mr Clarke might run away and they proposed therefore to take him to an army hospital where he would be well looked after.

Clarke was in a terrible state, both physically and mentally. It didn't need a doctor to tell me that, and I was convinced that even the sight of a Gendarme would just about kill him. This was so clearly true that it seemed the obvious line to take. They knew their methods, and what they could do to a man. I put it to them on these lines. They had released him because he was very ill and they feared that he might die. If he should die whilst in their charge, people would think that it was because of some bad treatment he had received. This of course was not the case, he had some physical sickness. Nevertheless he was very dangerously ill and had also some mental sickness which had made him very much afraid of going back to Bridge House. I was sure that if they took him back he would die, which was what they were trying to avoid. I suggested that we call Dr Gauntlett down to confirm my opinion.

Gauntlett when brought down took his cue admirably. They finally agreed to phone Headquarters for a decision.

'OK, Clarke can stop, but these two men must stay in room to watch.'

This was almost as bad. I really did believe that the mere sight of a Gendarme would put the finishing touch to him.

After much argument they finally agreed to keep watch from the room next door to Clarke's on my undertaking to be responsible for the cost of the room and their meals. I was very pleasantly surprised at their agreement to this and at their undertaking to do everything possible to keep out of Clarke's sight. They remained there for many weeks, keeping watch, turn and turn about and faithfully stuck to their undertaking to keep out of sight. I don't think that Clarke ever knew that they were there until all danger of his return to Bridge House appeared to have passed.

It was nearly midnight when I got home. Murray Rose and Trude (my children's nurse and now our housekeeper) were worried stiff. They had phoned all the likely places without getting news of me and had practically decided that I must be where in fact I had been, in Bridge House.

The next morning at about 8.30 a.m. Jones and I called on Fontanel as arranged. Kobelt and Schilling were there. Fontanel's first question naturally was about the events of the preceding evening. I explained that we had collected Clarke from Bridge House and had taken him to the Country Hospital, but that we had been compelled to give an undertaking to give no information. Although this undertaking might be regarded as having been given under duress, I had too healthy a regard for my own skin to run the risk of breaking it. Although I thought that Jones felt the same way about it, he told Fontanel that Clarke was in a terrible state and that he had obviously been very badly treated. I butted in quickly and said that I preferred not to have the matter pursued, since there was no effective action that we could take, and that I was only too pleased that the Gendarmerie had sufficient trust in my given word to ask me to undertake this kind of dirty work for them. We turned to other business and I thought no more of it.

At about eleven that morning I received a call from the Gendarmerie asking me to go round immediately to see Lt. Kawai. I went straight round to Hamilton House. Kawai was not there but was expected back shortly and I was asked to wait. It was a cold blustery day with a bitter north wind blowing. The waiting room was bare and unheated and after half an hour or so I began to feel chilly. I had a lot of work to do, so I went to the outer office where there was a receptionist in uniform and suggested that I came back later. He said that Kawai would not be long and I might as well wait. After another hour I went out again, cold and angry. I simply could not afford to waste time like this, but this time the receptionist had changed his role. I was told quite unmistakably that I had to wait, however long Kawai took.

Now I began to get really worried. Kawai obviously wanted to see me very badly and had given orders that I was to be sent for and held until he arrived. It could be no ordinary matter, but I could not think what could be on his mind.

Two o'clock came and I had been waiting nearly three hours. Shortly after that, standing at the window looking out over Kiangse Road, I saw a long black Gendarmerie car pull up at the door. A few minutes later I was sent for.

Kawai was sitting at the desk, looking as black as thunder, an interpreter standing at his side. I was not asked to sit down. Kawai barked in Japanese, the interpreter translated.

'Lt. Kawai wants to know why you told lies to the Swiss Consul-General about Mr Clarke, after you had been ordered to say nothing.'

This was going to be tough.

'I don't understand. I have talked to no one. Why is this charge made?'

'Don't lie to me. You know that you saw the Swiss Consul this morning. You reported to him, and he has made a complaint to the Japanese Consul-General.'

This really bowled me over. How on earth could Fontanel have done this after the warnings that we had given him? Thank goodness I was not the one who gave the show away. At least I had nothing to hide so far as I was concerned.

'I gave my word to say nothing to anyone. I was warned that if I spoke out of turn, I should be sent to Bridge House myself. I don't want to go there, as you must realize, and I have therefore not talked.'

'Then how did the Swiss Consulate know? Someone must have talked, either you or Mr Jones. You are the responsible one.'

Accusation and denial continued for the best part of an hour with no sign of a let up, Kawai still tearing mad. No doubt he had been severely ticked off by his own senior officer and was going to take it out on somebody's hide. I reminded him that I had been at the Swiss Consulate when I received the first message from the Gendarmerie and that I had borrowed their car. I had told them then why I wanted the car, so that they knew that much from me. Mr Clarke was a well-known man and we had driven through the streets of Shanghai to the hospital lobby. When we arrived, there had been people in the lobby, any one of these might have reported to the Swiss Consulate.

I had been cold and shivering when the interview started. I was now in a sweat as well and felt colder than ever. I had eaten only a hurried light breakfast nearly eight hours ago and was beginning to feel weak on my pins.

I could see no sign of relenting on the brutal, angry face of Kawai until I tried again the youth, innocence and inexperience line, with slight variations. I reminded him that I had no past experience of public affairs to help me through the very difficult job that I was now trying to do, that my job was to do all that I could to help the British Community collectively, or as individuals, such as Mr Clarke, and that I knew that my only hope of being able to do so lay in playing fair with the Japanese authorities, as I had most emphatically done in this case.

When Kawai spoke directly to me in English for the first time since I had entered the room, I knew that the battle was won, for the moment at any rate.

'When I came here, I had decided to send you to Bridge House to take the place of Mr Clarke. Now I think perhaps you tell me the truth. We will see. You may go now.'

I was reprieved for the time being, but I knew that it would mean a black mark against me in the Gendarmerie records. I wasn't greatly surprised therefore when Wallis of the Confederation Life asked me to call on him in his office some weeks later. I knew that he had been working for the Embassy in the Recruiting Office, and suspected that this had served as a cover for other work. He told me that he had heard from a reliable source that I was on the list for Bridge House. He felt it only fair to warn me so that I might make what preparations I could. He was sure of his information, although of course there was no telling when the arrest would occur.

This sort of thing was definitely getting me down. I had for some time past had everything arranged in the office so that my sudden departure, if it occurred, would cause as little disturbance as possible to the administration of the B.R.A. affairs. All that I could do so far as my personal comfort was concerned, was to put a selection of my warmest clothes by the bedside each night so that I should at least have something warm in which to start my sojourn in the place of meditation. It is perhaps not to be wondered at that whilst I waited at home in the evenings, every ring of the doorbell or telephone, or every step on the gravel made me jump perceptibly in my chair and left me in a cold sweat. I really was getting nervy.

They called for a British Engineer. He went into the bathroom to fetch some toilet articles and committed suicide rather than go to Bridge House. K.M. Anderson, the President of the American Association, was picked up one night and taken off. He was only in Bridge House for two days and I believe that his early release was due to the intervention of the Japanese Consulate. Would my turn be next?

This state of uncertainty and fear continued for weeks and months. My own uncertainties were partially relieved by the early summer. One day Anderson and I were asked to go to the Gendarmerie Office at Hamilton House. We were shown to a waiting room and asked to sit down. Sato came out of a neighbouring room, and through the open door we could see a long table at which were seated a dozen or so men in uniform, with Kawai at the head of the table. Sato greeted us, exchanged a few words, asked us to wait, and returned to the other room.

'I think this is it', said Anderson.

'What?'

'I heard that they were going to hold a special conference to decide whether or not to allow the Associations to carry on. If not, they will send us to B.H.'

He would not tell me how he knew. He could be pretty secretive at times. So we waited, very unhappily. After an hour or so, Sato appeared again, all smiles. He was carrying a basket of Chinese Mandarin oranges. He offered us one each, insisted on our taking them and said:

'No need to wait any more. Goodbye', and bowed. Maybe Anderson was right. It was a peculiar incident however you looked at it. But I didn't go to B.H. and there did seem to be a perceptible easing of surveillance from then on.

8

THE RELIEF EFFORT

Aʟᴛʜᴏᴜɢʜ our initial relief problem was not great, it soon became apparent that we must visualize a time when the majority of the community would exhaust their resources and be in need of help. We had therefore to start building an organization which would be capable of expanding to deal with a problem of this magnitude. This called for a first class organizer who would be able to devote his whole time to it, and so leave me free to deal with questions of organization, and political problems in general. We were fortunate in getting G.E. Marden to take on the job. He had a knack for getting the right people to work for him, and he also had an enormous knowledge of human nature in general, and that of Shanghailanders in particular.

The banks had all been taken over by the Japanese on the outbreak of war. They first froze all accounts, and later allowed drawings on current accounts to a maximum of $2,000 per month, irrespective of the family to be supported. In due course they also took over all the large companies and seized their stocks. Where the companies had liquid assets, payment of salaries was permitted, with a maximum of $2,000 per employee per month, provided that the employee was not also drawing on a bank account. At first, a small family could get by on this figure, but after a few weeks the Japanese declared that the Chinese dollar then current was no longer legal tender, and that it would be replaced by the dollar of the Nanking puppet government at the rate of two old dollars to one new one. This cut all bank accounts in half with the stroke of a pen, without there being, other than for a very brief period, a compensating increase in the purchasing power of the dollar.

Then came the wholesale replacement of British employees in official bodies such as the Chinese Maritime Customs, and the Shanghai Municipal Council, and reduction of staff in utility companies such as the power, waterworks, and telephone companies.

At the same time the Japanese were ordering that certain realizable personal assets such as motor cars, firearms, radios, cameras and binoculars must be surrendered without compensation. Hotels and apartment houses were commandeered and occupants were rarely permitted to remove furniture or even, in some cases, personal effects. We were being beggared very rapidly and efficiently.

The relief organization grew very rapidly and became a very efficient if not exactly popular body. We took a very serious view of our duties, believing that whilst our primary function was to help those in need, we should do so at the lowest possible cost to the British government and British people. Much of what was spent would be irrecoverable. It behoved us therefore to support ourselves for as long as we could, and to stave off the day when we should have to call for remittances from home. This meant that we should give aid only to those genuinely in need, and that on the lowest scale compatible with the maintenance of good health and reasonable well-being.

We initiated a comprehensive drive for funds. Raising money at a time like this is not easy, and is a real test of generosity. The response was really surprising. We obtained cheques on personal accounts in sterling, which we sold on the local market. We continued to do this even after the Japanese declared such transactions illegal, but had to exercise the greatest caution. It also led to some difficulties in explaining to the Japanese where our funds came from, but we were able to fake our records to make it appear that the Swiss Consulate was the source.

In order to avoid wasteful expenditure of our resources, we had to make careful investigations into the means of those who applied for help. We deliberately bore down rather heavily in the early days in order to discourage people from coming to us whilst they still had other means of support. We urged all those in need to support themselves for as long as they could by sale of surplus personal effects in the belief that sooner or later we should be interned, repatriated, or ejected from our homes and would lose all that we could not carry. Our actions may have been drastic, and I was truly sorry for those who suffered unduly by them, but the result was that it was ten months before we had to touch a penny of outside money.

Our position was not made easier by the Japanese supervision of correspondence and ban on public meetings which made it impossible to explain fully to the community just what we were doing and why. I tried to counter this by setting up a propaganda division which naturally had to operate very much on the quiet. I would hold small meetings of a dozen or so selected individuals, explain to them what we were doing, and ask them to pass the word round as widely as possible. My propagandists would tell me what views and criticisms were being expressed. This was crucial, since I was fully occupied during the day, and the closing of all clubs and the difficulty of moving about cut off all normal channels through which one could keep a finger on the pulse of public feeling.

There was no room in my office for the relief section proper so space was found in the cathedral compound. We were eventually using everything but the cathedral itself, and it became a veritable community centre, with even a library, a grocer's shop, shoe shop, and tailor. We also organized free medical and dental attention for those unable to pay. We were finally able to provide practically everything the individual required from birth to burial. There was a tremendous amount of work involved, but there were so many people whose normal occupations had ceased, who were only to glad to have something constructive to do, that there was never any lack of volunteers.

There were, of course, also many Indians in Shanghai, principally Sikhs, who had come originally for service with the police, and a fair sized business community who were mainly Hindus. As there were so many of them and they needed different treatment, we decided to set up a separate relief organization to care for them. This was organized at the Union Church by Dr Tocher, a medical missionary. I had not previously had much contact with Indians in Shanghai. I found that even at a time like this when many were in extreme need, our efforts to assist them were consistently hampered by a series of petty squabbles based mainly on factional jealousy. On several occasions we had to suspend relief for a few days in order to allow tempers to cool, and on one occasion, to give us time to repair the damage resulting from a riot.

There were a few Indians who threw in their lot with the Japanese and they tried to edge into the relief organization in order to get control of the disbursement of relief funds and thereby control the Indian community. At this time the renegade Subbhas Chandra Bhose was being made much of in Japan, and was trying to recruit Indians in Shanghai and Malaya for the Free Indian Army. We were particularly anxious to continue the payment of relief to all Indians in distress in Shanghai in order that they might not be forced to join this army.

When the pro-Japanese elements failed to gain control of the relief organization, another trick was tried. I was sent for by Banjo, the Japanese Vice-Consul principally concerned with contact with the enemy communities. He told me I must stop giving assistance or relief to the Indians.

I was in general able to take a much stronger line with the Japanese Consulate than with any branch of the armed forces. There was a great deal of jealousy between the various branches of the occupying forces and they very seldom worked closely together. The Consulate had no forces with which to back up its orders, so that these could be largely disregarded until it was obvious that there was backing from local forces, at which time we had to give in, and quickly. I therefore protested this order on the grounds that the Indians were British subjects, and that relief funds were made available for them by the British Government for disbursement through the B.R.A. Banjo replied that India now came within the East Asia Company Prosperity Sphere of influence, and that the Japanese would look after them. I managed to prolong the argument for some weeks but realized that I should eventually be forced to give way. Chandra Bhose must have his recruits, and the Japanese propaganda department must have its photographs of Shanghai Indians flocking to join the Free Indian flag. Realizing the inevitable outcome, I arranged to transfer the disbursement of Indian relief to the Swiss Consulate. The Japanese could not give orders to them as they could to me.

We also looked after the Iraqis for a time. As a gesture of friendship, Great Britain had undertaken to provide certain consular services for this small community, so they naturally turned to the B.R.A. when our consular staff were interned. We were able to help them until the Japanese instructed them not to come to us anymore. However, the chairman of their relief organization, Mr Hayim, maintained surreptitious contact with me throughout.

I also had many problems of a personal nature to deal with. One woman asked me if I could give her a divorce from her husband. I explained that whilst I was willing to try almost anything once, this was something that I really couldn't do. She was most unwilling to accept my refusal, and said that she was satisfied that I could do anything, and would be quite satisfied with a divorce pronounced by me.

One of my most difficult purely personal problems concerned one Tewfik Pasha. Of slight build, with a long black beard, and invariably carrying a rusty umbrella, he spoke practically no English and somewhat schoolboy French in which language we conversed. When I learned his business, I was very glad that he could not speak English, and that Kira, my Japanese Navy Supervisor, had no French.

Tewfik told me that in the course of his past activities, he had run up against T.E. Lawrence. I had a copy of 'The Seven Pillars of Wisdom' and found a reference to one Tewfik Pashar who had been engaged in some sort of gun-running expedition. More recently, he had been sent to Japan as a representative of a Middle Eastern state. The outbreak of war had made it impossible for him to receive funds from his government and he was soon penniless. The Japanese had seized the opportunity to try to persuade him to work for them. He did not want to and had managed to get to Shanghai with his wife and two children. Here the Japanese were renewing their pressure and it was now a question of working for them or starving, unless support was forthcoming from some other source. For himself, he said he would cheerfully starve rather than work for the Japanese, but he could not see his children suffer. He brought the children to see me and they were positively beautiful. It may have been good showmanship, but it was certainly effective, I couldn't see them starve either.

Tewfik of course had no claim on the British, in fact he volunteered the information that he had always been anti-British and had fought against them. But there was no doubt in his mind that he was infinitely more anti-Japanese than anti-British. I knew that his assertion that the Japanese were trying to use him for propaganda purposes was correct, just as they were trying to get control of my Indians, and had taken the Iraqi's out of my hands. It was clearly part of the Axis strategy to meet in the Near East and the connecting route lay through India, Iraq and Trans-Jordan. My duty as a British subject clearly lay therefore in trying to enable Tewfik to keep clear of the Japanese. On the other hand, there was the risk that if they caught me at it, not only would my number be up, but it might also prejudice the work of the Association. I consulted J.R. Jones who agreed that I should help Tewfik, but that I should have to be very discreet. I therefore paid him out of my 'slush' fund, a sum of money made up of my own funds and money which I had under my personal control for emergency needs, for which I was not called upon to account to anybody. The main difficulty, or so I thought, was that the Japanese would wonder what he was living on. Actually, my chief worry was Tewfik himself. He simply had no sense of discretion and would wander into my office at all hours of the day, to my very great embarrassment.

9

REPATRIATION FOR THE FEW

SPRING arrived and passed and summer heat began. Life began to look pretty grim. Gone were our hopes for a quick finish to the war. The news had given us a series of jolting shocks, very lowering to our morale, esteem and national pride.

First came the fall of Hong Kong where nearly all of us had friends; then the sinking of HMS *Repulse* and HMS *Prince of Wales*; then came the fall of Manila and Singapore itself which all had thought impregnable against anything the Japanese could produce. The long-drawn heroic struggle on Bataan then culminated in the fall of Corregidor. How the Japanese played it up in the local press and radio! At first we were frankly sceptical, it just could not be true, but we finally had to accept the bitter truth. Where now was the vaunted supremacy of the white man?

Things weren't going well in the West either. General Rommel had retaken Tobruk and the whole of Libya, and was knocking on the gates of Egypt. This was going to be a long, long war. The West would have to be cleared up before forces of any size could be spared to deal with the Japanese. The tide had not even begun to turn yet and even the most optimistic of rational thinkers could not envisage a conquering army coming to our rescue in less than a period of years.

Money was increasingly scarce, and accommodation was becoming crowded. The currency was depreciating and prices rising to what even then seemed to be fantastic levels. Gone altogether was the luxurious living of the past. We could not afford to keep our former number of servants. Women were having to do tasks which, whilst commonplace in the homeland, were far more onerous under the conditions of life in a tropical climate where the layout of dwellings and whole economy of European life was designed on the premise of a virtually unlimited supply of cheap domestic help.

In spite of the bad news and our own many difficulties we were not utterly despondent. One great hope buoyed us up, one word — REPATRIATION. It was the cheering song in everyone's heart. Our government would send big ships to take us all away. Ships were short of course, but there were many more Japanese in Canada, the States, Australia, India, positive hosts of them all over the East. The Japanese would want them back too, particularly for the information that they could give. We were simply bound to be repatriated. There were also all the Embassy and Consular staffs to be exchanged. They would go first of course. There were not enough of them to fill a ship and probably a favoured few would get away with them. It was a bit surprising that they had not gone already but no doubt it was taking a little time to get the procedure arranged, after which it would just be a question of following out a tested routine until we were away.

I, of course, being in constant contact with the Swiss Consulate, knew that negotiations for repatriation were going on and that snags were being slowly ironed out. Numbers were fixed and a tentative date mentioned. There would be so many places for British, so many for Dutch, so many for other nationals. These figures had again to be subdivided by countries, that is, from Japan, China proper, Hong Kong, Malaya and so on.

When we had obtained the figure for China and had deducted the official personnel, we could see how many civilian places were left and decide on the fairest method of allocation. In the meantime, the local Japanese Consular officials took a hand in the arrangements without any reference whatever to the Swiss Consulate or to us. They issued instructions that large numbers of enemy nationals in interior points and various outports should be brought to Shanghai in readiness for repatriation. We heard nothing of it until these people were on the point of departure!

The Swiss Consulate and ourselves protested energetically, both locally and through Tokyo. The allocation of places to British civilian personnel was a matter for the accredited representatives of the British Government to decide after due reference to the Home authorities, and the Japanese had no right whatever to attempt to force their choice on us in this manner. We would not be so forced and would place solely on the Japanese the responsibility of housing and feeding these people on arrival in Shanghai and we would give no undertaking that any of them would be repatriated on the forthcoming steamer. They were extremely angry at what they appeared to consider unwarranted interference on our part and said that their arrangements were far too far advanced to permit any change being made.

It was all very well for us to say that we would accept no responsibility for these people from the outports if the Japanese insisted on bringing them to Shanghai, but we could not in fact leave them to the tender mercies of the Japanese. They had apparently not considered how they would be lodged and fed, muttered something vague about hotels which were already full to overflowing, and had no constructive ideas. We therefore suggested that if they would provide suitable premises, and would put up the necessary funds, the B.R.A. would set up the necessary organization for management and care. After some haggling this was agreed and they made the Columbia Country Club available to us and we settled on a reasonable sum for initial expenses and for maintenance. Arrangements at the Country Club were most efficiently made by H.F. Gardner of the Asiatic Petroleum Co. assisted by Carlisle and King of the Customs. The Columbia Club was a delightful place, and was to become later on the pick of the internment camps and as such was reserved for the sick and for families with very young children.

The would-be repatriates arrived and settled in before we knew what the China repatriation quota would be and how many of them would ultimately be allowed to go. There was tremendous disappointment and anxiety among them when they learned that their departure was definitely uncertain and many were the special, oh so special reasons presented to me as to why this or that person should receive preferential treatment.

The ship on which the repatriation took place will always be known to the Shanghai public as '*Wangle Maru*' instead of *Kamakura Maru* more in sorrow than in anger when it was found that less than two hundred places in all were allotted to Shanghai. It was entirely out of proportion to the number of British nationals there as compared with those from outports.

The allotment was divided into certain categories having equal priority, the numbers to go under each category being specified by the British Government. This greatly simplified what is, under the best of circumstances, a very difficult task. The Swiss Consulate selected those people who would come under the categories of former inmates of Bridge House and employees of the Chinese Government or semi-officials such as members of the Customs service and Municipal Council. They asked the B.R.A. to make recommendations under the categories of women whose husbands were already out of China in one of the services, or people deemed of value to the war effort, whilst a panel of British doctors was asked to choose those who came under the final category, the sick and the aged.

The other part of the story was the Embassy and Consular list, which did include some unexpected names. When their officials were interned, each senior member was asked to submit to the Japanese a list of all those in their respective services, together with their dependents. The officials thought that it would be a good thing to include as many names as possible, including those of many temporary and even part-time employees, in order that these people might enjoy such measure of diplomatic protection as this listing might afford. It would for instance prevent their being picked up for questioning by the Gendarmerie. From this point of view it was a wise action, but when it came to the question of repatriation there was a great deal of understandable heartburning at seeing numbers of Shanghai flappers, who had been doing temporary secretarial work at an Embassy or Consulate, going gaily up the gangplank at the expense of worthier people. There was, of course, some wangling in the Embassy lists, such as the well-known society lady who went as nurse to the children of a certain European Consul-General.

There was one job that gave me real pleasure in all this, and that was calling up the wives of serving husbands. Three of us divided the names amongst us and started about four o'clock on Friday afternoon to invite people to sail on Tuesday. I got a real kick out of their expressions of pleasure, astonishment, dismay at the packing to be got through and so on. Some were voluble, some incoherent, some in a complete flap. To those who had no close friends to turn to for help, we sent willing volunteers.

There was a last minute hitch in the first category on the list, those who had been in Bridge House. The Gendarmerie had recently picked up Brown, an engineer who had come out to the Shanghai Power Co. in order to install a high pressure boiler of a new revolutionary type. Presumably the Japanese were not sure what made the wheels go round and they wanted to squeeze the information out of Brown before he left. He presumably was proving stubborn about it since the Gendarmes held on to him until the very last moment and it was only on the threat of calling off the whole repatriation that he was finally released.

The *Kamakura Maru* left on 17 August 1942, a sweltering summer day. I was on the wharf at Pootung to help check the repatriates through. I spent about five hours under a corrugated iron roof lining up the queues, checking papers, carrying babies and baggage and saying goodbye to friends. I was soaked through after the first ten minutes and found it pretty hard to be cheerful at seeing so many friends go when I wanted so much to go myself.

I went to say goodbye to Tony George who had come on board separately. I found him in a small cabin with three other Consuls-General.

They were gravely deciding the allocation of berths by seniority, but there seemed to be a diplomatic argument as to whether seniority for this purpose went by years of service or port standing. George was not a happy man. I had been able to persuade him to come to my house several times for an hour or so during the period of his internment, ostensibly for a game of tennis, but actually to get his advice on various matters. He seemed to feel that he had not done all that he could have done although he was never very specific as to the particular direction in which his efforts had not satisfied him. I think he would have liked to remain with us in Shanghai, had not diplomatic usage precluded such action. I cannot compare him with other Consuls-General in Shanghai. There was nothing in my life to bring me into close contact with his predecessors. I only know that to me he was the soul of courtesy and helpfulness, both personally and in my official capacity. He was never too busy to see me, and never failed to discuss fully the point at issue, to appreciate my point of view, and to co-operate to the fullest extent when his help was needed.

10

RESTRICTIONS AND PRIVATIONS

MARDEN and J.R. Jones of the B.R.A. had sailed away on the *Kamakura*. Adamson of the Hongkong Bank became Vice-Chairman and Bill Braidwood joined the Executive Committee as a kind of special assistant to me. As his company, the China Soap Co., had virtually closed work, Bill was able to devote practically the whole of his time to the B.R.A. He loved organization, and would illustrate his ideas in graph form with squares and circles and arrows, and connecting lines in all directions. I thought him at first a bit of an idealist but there was good common sense behind it all. I was the plodder of the team, almost overcome by his brilliance. He took so much work off my hands that I even had time to sit down and think.

The Representative of the American Red Cross in China, Anderson, President of the American Association, had also been repatriated. His place was taken by Anker Bailey Henningsen. Anker, as we soon came to call him, was a gem. He was a business man, ruthless in the American style where business was concerned, making up his mind what he wanted or what had to be done, and going after it tooth and nail, impatient of opposition, harsh to incompetence, and withall a delightful friend. From the time of his taking over, the co-operation between the two Associations became about as close and cordial as it was possible to be.

Bill and I often lunched with Anker, his personal assistant Bill Gray and Jimmy Nichols, Vice-President of the American Association. Over sandwiches and coffee, we would discuss the affairs of the day and compare notes, and in this way kept the activities of the two associations working on parallel lines.

The Americans had tackled the relief problem on rather different lines from us. Almost from the outset they converted the American School premises into a hostel and opened a food distribution centre in a garage on Avenue Foch. They felt that it would have to be done sooner or later, so they might as well start immediately in order to get over the headaches of organization before the situation became acute. We believed it would not be wise to start this form of relief too soon. Our problem from the point of view of numbers was so much greater than the Americans that it was essential our people should exhaust every means of supporting themselves before they came to us for anything more than financial help. We felt that had we set up hostels in the early days they would have been filled immediately since the individual would have seen in them the easiest solution to their problem and would not have made a serious effort to work out their own salvation. The Americans found this happening, and there were cases of people selling up their homes and going to live at the school. It did not worry the American Association unduly because the school was big enough to accommodate all the Americans who were likely to need to take advantage of it. However, there were no places available to us which could house our six thousand.

The American Association also handled their financial relief much more simply. Any American citizen who wanted it could apply for and receive financial help. In our case, applicants had to prove their need and the extent of it. We set up an elaborate organization under the control of A.V.T. Dean of Butterfield and Swire to determine the cost of living and this represented the maximum scale, exclusive of rent, on which relief payments were made. Nor did applicants receive the full amount unless they had no other source of income. It would have been far easier and simpler to follow the American plan, and would have saved us a great deal of unpopularity. We felt, nevertheless, that our prime duty in affording relief was to do so as economically as possible. There was one feature of this which was of considerable concern and which cast doubt in our own minds as to the wisdom of our policy. We all believed that, failing repatriation, there was a very tough time coming for the Allied communities in China. Which was the better alternative to follow — that of preparing people for it by starting the toughening process now, or that of providing the best that could be afforded now in order to give them some fat to fall back on in the lean days to come? It is still hard to say, even after the event. I incline to believe that the line that we took was better and that it did teach many tricks and wrinkles of economy that helped to ease the shock of internment.

We were greatly helped in our relief effort by the allocation to us of substantial quantities of cracked wheat and rice which had been sent by the American Red Cross. Originally intended for distribution to Chinese, it had perforce been left in Shanghai through lack of shipping facilities.

Under the terms of the gift, the wheat could not be sold. However, we needed money, money which had not been subscribed for relief purposes. For we had received a long cable from the British Government through the Swiss Consulate, in reply to ours outlining the situation, our present self-support policy, and our probable ultimate needs. In it our policy was approved and the Government promised to supply us with funds when needed, to be disbursed on certain defined lines, provided that our local contributions were made to conform to the same restrictions. We were never able to obtain a reason for this ruling but felt that we must conform to it.

One of the disbursement regulations was that no relief would be paid to British subjects of Chinese race, and although we protested that this would cause not only distress in certain special cases, but also serious loss of prestige, they would not alter the ruling. We assumed that the main reason was the relatively large number of Chinese who had acquired British nationality by the accident of birth in Hong Kong or Malaya, but who had never in any shape or form forsworn their Chinese birth or felt any allegiance to the British Crown.

We were most concerned about a number of students from Singapore whose forebears had for perhaps several generations been domiciled in Malaya. A number of these families habitually sent their sons to university in China. They were now cut off from friends, and many were in great distress. We felt that it would be a serious blow to British prestige if these youths were denied the assistance afforded to other British subjects, although the mere fact that they were sent to China to complete their education indicated that their families still had close affiliations with the land of their origin. We decided to do what we could to use other means to help them, and the cracked wheat served this purpose well.

We made the wheat available for free distribution at a certain rate per person per month, but asked all those who could afford to do so to make voluntary contributions at a rate suggested. A large portion of the recipients elected to make the donations as suggested. This provided funds to help these British subjects of Chinese race, and other special cases whom strict adherence to the letter of the law would have forced us to turn away. It was really rather appropriate that the cracked wheat originally intended for Chinese in distress should eventually come back to them in this way.

Although we were settling into our routine, our problems were steadily becoming more complex as the scope of relief had to be enlarged to take care of ever increasing numbers. Housing, clothing, feeding, medical, dental and hospital services, transport, and almost every aspect of daily life of the individual now became items for which we had to make provision.

We also started a complete classification of the whole British community, cross-indexing all qualifications so that when the next repatriation boat came, we could pick out any conceivable classifications, at a moment's notice. Since this involved the recording of much confidential information, we opened an office at the Swiss Consulate. Rutherford took charge, with Captain Muton, a marine shipmaster, looking after the classification of people with technical qualifications. I mention Muton particularly, because after my internment he was hauled in by the Gendarmerie and handled very roughly indeed on account of the work he had done there. I am pretty sure they extracted nothing from him, he looked so bad when he came out.

That autumn was fairly humdrum. We were forced to wear numbered red armbands. In a spirit of bravado, I chose to wear armband No. 1. Having got us tabbed, we were refused entry to all public places of amusement, to all cinemas, nightclubs, hotels and restaurants. Not that by that time many of us had the money to spend on these forms of relaxation, but it was none the less galling for that.

When the Japanese had taken over the Settlement, they had instructed us to continue our normal avocations. It took us a little time to settle down to this, and as far as I was concerned, my activities were anything but normal. However, the Amateur Dramatic Company decided to take them at their word and put on a show. To be on the safe side, they approached various authorities until they found one who was sufficiently interested to give them the go-ahead, with the sole proviso that the script be submitted and approved before the show was staged.

E.G. Smith-Wright was then the leading light in the A.D.C. He was in the first rank both as a producer and actor, and was no mean hand with the pen. After some deliberation they picked Richard III, principally I fancy, because Smith-Wright wanted to play the hunchback king. They were right in assuming that in the case of that well-known playwright William Shakespear-San, the script would be approved without comment. The play was put on to large and enthusiastic audiences, including many Japanese. Smith-Wright, always superb, surpassed himself. There were glowing notices in the Japanese controlled press. After two performances, the theatre was closed down by order of the Japanese Gendarmerie, everything was plastered with seals, and the doors were guarded by troops with fixed bayonets.

I was sent for by Ohba, special assistant at Naval Headquarters. Ohba-San had recently been taking an indecent and very unwelcome interest in the affairs of the Association. He did not seem to be satisfied with the supervision exercised by our tiny playboy Kira. In this he was undoubtedly justifed. Ohba had been to Oxford and Harvard. One gathered that in neither place had his views on life been properly appreciated, and he was a very embittered, anti-British and anti-American young man. He had at least learned to speak perfect English and American, for he understood pretty well the nuances of the slang of both countries. Such people can be very awkward customers, he was just gloating over the heaven-sent opportunity to repay one hundredfold the slights that his *amour propre* had suffered in both countries. It was a very real thing to him, and I regarded him as one of the most dangerous people we had to deal with.

Ohba sent for me, and Ohba received me, looking as though he had just turned over a large rock and was about to enjoy squashing the slug that emerged bewildered from beneath it.

'The Commander-in-Chief of the Japanese Naval Forces wishes to have your explanation as to why you permitted the Amateur Dramatic Company to produce a play which contained many anti-Japanese sentiments.'

I was completely floored. I had been so busy that I had hardly noticed the show was on. I had certainly not had time to go and see it. The A.D.C. had done their own negotiating with the authorities, which suited me very well, and I had not regarded their activities as any concern of mine. I told Ohba this and added that I assumed the production had been duly approved by the appropriate authority and that in any case I did not understand how the production of the three-hundred-year-old classic, and Shakespeare at that, could prove offensive to the Japanese.

'Mr Collar, you are not taking this sufficiently seriously. It is a very serious matter indeed, it is useless to indulge in quibbles. Mr Smith-Wright deliberately emphasized the imperialistic flavour of some of his speeches with the object of inflaming his British audience against the Japanese and thus provoking serious anti-Japanese incidents. The British members of the audience applauded these speeches very loudly indeed. The most serious view is taken of this matter in the very highest circles. You are responsible.'

It was laughable all right, particularly if Smith-Wright had been trying to put one over, but Ohba was making anything but a laughing matter of it for me. He was going to make me treat it seriously, whether I wanted to or not. I finally obtained permission to see Smith-Wright before going further into the matter.

Smith-Wright had already been on the mat with Ohba and was about as dumbfounded as I was. The play had been properly approved by the Japanese censor and he swore that he had not played any tricks with his rendering of it. We saw Ohba again in due course and presented our defence. This was received and recorded with due gravity and undue hauteur, and we were told that the case would be carefully considered and we should hear further in due course. There was nothing more that we could do but sit back and await developments.

A few days later we were ordered to present ourselves at the Naval Landing-Party Headquarters. We were received by Ohba, and ushered into a room in which the only furniture consisted of a long conference table with chairs only on the side away from us.

'You will stand thus, at attention', said Ohba, placing us together. 'Face this door. When the court comes in, you will bow. When the court takes its place at the table, you will turn and face them, bow again, and return to the position of attention.'

I did not like the sound of 'the court'. It looked as though the molehill had produced a real mountain. However, 'When in Rome do as the Romans tell you' had been our motto for a long time. I know that my bow was not quite according to regulations. I was too much dazzled by the display of brass that came through the door, dazzled and definitely worried too. First a general, with ADC, a full admiral with ditto, then, most sinister, a lieutenant of Gendarmerie, Kawai, all girt with the panoply of war.

There was a sword on the table with hilt or point towards us to indicate the verdict. Certain formalities were gone through in Japanese and Ohba read from a long document. When he had finished, he turned to us and said: 'I will now translate the verdict of this court into English. One, the Lyceum Theatre shall be closed. All the properties therein shall be sealed and kept in the custody of the Japanese forces until the conclusion of hostilities. Two, the A.D.C. shall be dissolved and shall not be permitted to produce any more plays. Three, Mr Collar and Mr Smith-Wright shall write an apology to the Japanese forces for their anti-Japanese activities. Four, Mr Collar shall be responsible for seeing that these orders are properly carried out and shall accept responsibility for the future actions of all members of the A.D.C. This is the verdict of this court.'

That was all. The court rose, we bowed; the court walked out, we bowed. Ohba walked out, we walked out; we looked for a drink. I forget whether we found one.

11
IMPRISONMENT

BY the time November 1942 came I was wearing pretty thin. I had
lost 23 lbs. in weight and the heat of that Shanghai summer was not
the principal cause. The strain of constant negotiations with the Japanese
authorities and the nagging uncertainty over the possibility of being
caught out some day had reduced my nerves to rags. When the blow
finally fell, it snapped my last few threads of control.

It came at some time before dawn on 5 November. I heard the sound
of booted feet on the gravel outside the house. No other sound would
have awakened me, but this was the one I had been expecting for months.
There were muttered words, then the sound of feet walking round the
side of the house. I heard the bamboo gate creak open, then footsteps
on the lawn under my window. Sentries on guard at the back, others
waiting at the front door, giving the watchers time to cover all possible
exists. Then came a prolonged ring on the bell and a banging on the
door. I lay still, pretending to myself that I was still asleep. Shouts added
to the noise of the bell and hammering. There were three of us in the
house, my good friend Murray Rose, Trude, and I. I have never been
so ashamed of anything as the fact that I lay there and let Trude get
up to go down to the door. She stopped at the door of my room and said:

'There is someone at the door, shall I go down and see who it is?'

I said 'Yes', being quite sure who it was, but still trying to believe
it was no concern of mine and to force myself back to sleep. I couldn't
keep it up for long. Heavy boots trod the uncarpeted stairs then came
into my room. Straight into my eyes shone the beams of two powerful
torches.

'Are you Mr H. Collar?'

'Yes, what do you want?'

'You get up, come with us. Please read', pushing a paper under my
nose.

It was a mimeographed order of some kind; and, although brief, it
took me several minutes to read it. Even then I did not grasp it properly.

Something about being taken away and looked after, all for my protection. It did not sound quite like Bridge House, the house of torture, but I was too dazed to comprehend it properly. Then they asked me:

'Mr A. M. Rose also live here?'

'Yes.'

'Where is he now?'

'Upstairs as far as I know.'

'You take us to him.'

I crawled off the bed, my knees completely devoid of power and dragged myself upstairs. Murray was still in bed.

'They want you too Murray', and that was the last I remember for quite a time. I passed out completely for the first, and so far the last, time in my life. I didn't mean to do it but it was probably the best thing I could possibly have done. It gave the troop of guards such a shock that they treated me with quite exceptional consideration.

They carried me downstairs and put me back on my bed and the next thing I remember it was full dawn and there were four Gendarmes standing round me with very worried expressions on their faces. I started to raise myself and was immediately pushed back.

'Not to hurry, please stay until well. After, you come with us.' That suited me. I asked for the pamphlet and had a good look at it. It didn't look so bad now. Being mimeographed, it was probably being widely used, and it seemed fairly clearly to be some form of concentration at a place in Haiphong Road. The phone beside my bed rang and I stretched an arm for it. I was immediately stopped.

'No, not permissible.' Stamped seals were slapped over the instrument.

Murray and Trude came in and asked if they could help. I should obviously have to get some packing done. Luckily I had for some months had a selection of apparel suitable for Bridge House kept ready in one drawer. I told them to get this out, give me what I needed to wear, and to pack the rest. The Gendarmes helped. When they had finished one of the Gendarmes turned and asked me:

'Is this all?'

'Yes.'

'Not enough, no blankets, everything too little, have more suitcase?'

'Yes, upstairs, near Mr Rose's room.'

'OK, I fetch,' and fetch he did, the largest one in the pile, a thing that I had always had difficulty in carrying unaided.

They filled it between them while I got up and tested out my legs. They seemed to be all right again and I thought I might take full advantage of their concern and try and get a wash and shave which I knew would make me feel better. They agreed, but would not trust me alone, they had lost their prisoners that way before. One of them accompanied me, kept a watchful eye on the business of shaving and politely turned his back when I made use of the toilet.

I could not manage my big bag, so one of them carried it downstairs for me. Not to be outdone in politeness another one picked up my small suitcase. The gardener and a friend arrived just as we went out by the door. They were promptly impressed into service and slung our three packages over their shoulders on a bamboo carrying pole. It was only then that we saw the full number of our captors. There were eight in all. It made us feel quite important.

It was raining lightly as we walked down the Crescent, our private road, and we saw the anxious faces of Butts, Hughes and Lowe peering through their windows as we passed. Out in Yu Yuen Road, we turned left and halted after about two hundred yards by a gate opposite a compound inhabited by the employees of a Japanese cotton mill. Here the gardener was chased away and I had to pick up both bags myself. It would have been undignified to be seen helping me in public. We walked up a lane and were ushered into a mat shed guarded by sentries.

There were half a dozen other men there who had been picked up in the neighbourhood. I did not know any of them. We sat around for half an hour or so and then one of them started talking in Chinese to one of the guards. The guard appeared fairly friendly, and the prisoner remarked that he had been made to leave in such a hurry that he had not had time to bring any money. The guard asked where he lived, and was told that he came from West Park Mansions, a bare three or four minutes walk away. We were apparently not due to leave for some time and the guard, possibly scenting a spot of profit for himself, obtained permission to escort the prisoner to his flat to collect the funds.

This seemed like a good idea and Murray obtained permission to do likewise. We both had a little money on us but Murray had some locked away which he had not cared to produce when we were arrested. I was more interested in the possibility of his collecting some food. It was past eight and we were getting hungry.

In ten minutes or so they were back, Murray with the pockets of his raincoat bulging widely. He just had time to tell me that he had collected a loaf and a piece of sausage that the cook had slapped together with a couple of fried egg sandwiches, when we were herded out into a waiting army truck. The truck went off full bat towards the west and then turned along Keswick Road towards the railway crossing. We started to speculate on our probable destination, guessing that it might be the Seventh Day Adventist Hospital on Rubicon Road. I knew that the Japanese had been inspecting it because I had looked it over myself as a possible hostel and had had an eye kept on it when they told me that I could not have it. It was a lovely spot and we were beginning to pat ourselves on the back when we turned east on Tunsin Road and stopped opposite the Daybrook estate.

Here we were joined by Phil Higgs of the Power Company, and after a long wait, by A. de C. Sowerby, the naturalist. He looked terribly ill and could barely drag himself along. A couple of us jumped off to help him up although the guards did not seem at all pleased about it, and lifted him bodily into the back of the truck. He was escorted by a senior NCO of the Gendarmerie with whom he had evidently been expostulating for some time, saying that he was absolutely unfit to be treated in this manner and that it would probably kill him. He was begging the Gendarme to telephone his headquarters to see if he could not be left in his home until he had been examined by a Japanese doctor, who would verify the fact of his unfitness. The sight of Sowerby being lifted into the truck and collapsing on the pile of luggage apparently convinced the Gendarme that he ought to do something about it. He had Sowerby lifted off the truck and escorted back to his home. This was a unique case. Other men were actually taken out of hospital and brought into camp, so seriously ill that they had to be sent back to hospital on the following day, but this time under constant guard in the hospital at the Ward Road Gaol.

This seemed to be our last port of call, and after Sowerby left we were whisked off into the town, finally stopping outside our future home in Haiphong Road.

It was the last many of us were to see of the outside world for two and a half years, Murray and I ate our fried egg sandwiches standing in the truck as it tore along the streets. They had been knocked together in haste and the yolk was very soft, it dribbled out of our mouths and down our chins. We had the feeling that appearances were not going to be very important from now on.

It was drizzling as we arrived alongside a high red wall and stopped outside the brick gatehouse. We were herded off the truck which immediately drove off for another load. Rows of soldiers blocked off the road on each side of the gate through which we straggled. We had no time to look round as we got inside. Sentries turned us to the left into a long wooden shed. There was quite a crowd of uniformed Japanese and a few in civilian clothes standing at the door of the shed, watching us go in and checking us off. Among them was Banjo of the Japanese Consulate with whom I had argued on more occasions than I cared to remember. When he recognized me in the slow-moving file he said:

'You here too, Mr Collar. I am very surprised to see you. I did not know anything about this until I was told to come here this morning. Mr Henningsen inside too. I will try to get you both out. I am sure it is a mistake.'

I filed on inside feeling somewhat cheered. I too was quite sure it was a mistake. The Japanese themselves couldn't get on without me.

The shed inside was fairly full and men continued to arrive. I was too tired and dispirited to talk to any of them. I managed to get my baggage against a wall and sat down on it leaning back with my eyes closed. From time to time somebody would come up and speak to me, but for most of the day I just sat there and dozed. This seemed to be the end of all my hard work and it was just too much.

We stood around without food or drink until well on into the afternoon. Then a Japanese in civilian clothes came in and harangued us in bad English for ten minutes, telling us we were being interned for our own protection, and the usual guff. After that we were told to pick up our baggage and to march into the main building. The room in which we were then crowded had a tiled floor, now covered in slimy mud. Over one of the doors was the wording 'V. D. Clinic'. Word was going round that this had once been a barracks of the US Marines. After milling round in here for an hour or so, space was cleared in the central doorway and a table set up. A young Japanese officer, in greatcoat and sword, shouted for silence and announced that a Colonel Odera would speak to us.

On to the table climbed a Japanese colonel, whose principal feature was a pair of flowing moustaches which earned him the instant nickname of 'Handlebars'. He made a speech in explosive Japanese sentences, translated to us in very bad English by the young lieutenant. I do not remember the exact form of it, but it was to the effect that we were now under military jurisdiction, that we should be treated well as long as we behaved well, but that if we didn't we should be for it. We should also be required to sign a paper after which we would be allotted rooms.

The lieutenant who then introduced himself as Lt. Honda read us a document which we were being asked, or rather instructed, to sign. It was a declaration to the effect that we would be good boys, the only paragraph of importance being the last one, announcing that we would make no attempt to escape. There was considerable demur over this, but we all, with one temporary exception, took the view that it was an undertaking given under duress and as such did not bind us. Everyone was too tired to argue by this time and we all passed up to the table to sign. After the signing was completed, signatures were counted and checked against the number of men on their lists. They checked and rechecked, and apparently decided that they had made no mistake and that they were one name short. Somebody had not signed, who was it? Nobody stepped forward. Very well, we would all be kept there whilst the complete list was checked against signatures and when the delinquent was found, it would be just too bad for him. At that, a short sandy-haired man shuffled forward and grinningly admitted that he was the missing man.

I recognized this Sandy as a man who had been in Bridge House and who on being released had come to the B.R.A. office and complained that we had done nothing to help him. We had not in fact known that he was there, but even then we had been getting food in fairly successfully. I think the reason was that he had been kept apart from the other British prisoners none of whom appeared to know anything about him when they came out.

He signed the document, saying that he might as well try it on to see whether he would be caught out or not. After what the Japanese had already done to him, he wasn't afraid of any more threats. This proved to be quite typical of the man. I think he was London born but Australian bred, and he had all the Cockney impudence and Australian independence and more besides of his own particular brand.

We were then allocated rooms. A Quartermaster stood at the door and called for ten men, six men, eight men, and as each batch formed up, they were led off by a soldier guide into the dark. Here and there two or three friends would try to keep together, but in the main, it was simply a question of the nearest men making requisite numbers for the next room. This resulted in rooms containing a complete and haphazard cross section of Shanghai society. Most of these rooms existed practically unchanged in personnel for the next two and a half years in spite of there being frequent opportunities to make changes. This always appeared to me remarkable and most interesting as an instance of how men of different ages, creeds, social status, education and ideals can settle down together, and not merely not want, but in most cases actually resist change. The only form of segregation that was made, and this was made by the Japanese themselves, was to allot different rooms to different

nationalities and this they insisted on. I would have much preferred to
see the nationalities also mixed and I am sure that this would have made
for better feeling throughout the camp. Murray and I kept together and
found ourselves allotted to a room on the first floor with twelve other
men. It was completely bare of furniture, but had a fireplace, and
windows to the south and west. Although we had not seen much of the
other rooms it looked as though we had not done too badly. We picked
a place against the inner wall, put down our baggage, and sat round
taking stock of each other. I noticed that Gordon was there, and Murray
found that he knew Blanks of the Mercantile Bank. R.J. Sheppard
(Shep.) had tacked on behind Murray and me which made three men
from ICI in this room.

We had not been there long when a Japanese came into the room asking
if I was there, saying that the Colonel wanted to see me downstairs.

'Aha', said I to Murray. 'This looks like where I get out. If I don't
get back for my baggage, you and Shep. can have it. You had better
keep my blankets anyway so get them taken out. I will try and come
up to see you before I go.'

Downstairs in the ill-lit hall, I found Henningsen waiting. He had
the same idea as I had. Banjo had also promised to get him out as soon
as possible. We were a little aggrieved that it had taken him so long.
Then the Colonel and Honda appeared.

'You are Mr Henningsen, President of the American Association?'

'Yes.'

'And you are Mr Collar, Chairman of the British Residents'
Association?'

'Yes.'

'Very well, Colonel Odera orders you to take charge of the interned
men in the camp. You, Mr Henningsen, will take charge of the
Americans, Dutch and Greeks. Mr Collar you will look after British
only, as there are so many British. Tomorrow we make full arrangements.
Just now, first thing, must appoint room captains, and make roll call.
We make roll call now.'

Henningsen and I fell over ourselves to say that we could not possibly
take charge here, they had better choose someone else who was going
to be permanently residing here. Mr Banjo had assured us that it was
all a mistake putting us in here and that he would arrange to have us
released immediately.

I felt that our protests were met with singular coolness. These soldier
blokes obviously didn't realize how important we were. They didn't

understand that we were accustomed to being insulted only by the very highest in Japanese officialdom, apart of course from the Gendarmerie. They would not take 'No' for an answer, so we reluctantly asked just what the requisite qualifications were for the room captains we had to appoint. From their replies we gathered that they meant room orderly: their principal duties would be those of fetching and carrying for the remainder, therefore we should choose men who were young and strong.

We then proceeded round the rooms, after first shouting ourselves hoarse telling everyone to try to get back where they started from. In each room the men had to line up and count off. We then picked out a strong, husky looking chap, preferably one whom we knew to be reliable, and appointed him room captain, telling him that we hoped shortly to call on him to come and collect food, eating utensils and blankets on behalf of his room. This took the best part of an hour, after which we were introduced to the kitchen and the mess hall. The food consisted of a number of Maxwell House tins labelled coffee but filled with a stew which we found afterwards had been made the day before by Bakerite, a local restaurant. There were a number of Chinese type brick stoves with iron pans on top in which we were told we could brew tea.

We went to the nearest room to collect some volunteer cooks and set them to trying to light fires. Straw appeared to be the only fuel, and damp straw at that. We could not issue the stew until the men had something to eat out of, so the distribution of rice bowls was the next job. These were issued out of a packing case, in accordance with the number of men each room captain said he had in his room. They were about as green as we were, but we were more interested in speed than in accuracy. We never did get the count right after that and were in continual trouble with the various quartermasters as they tried to check their stock records.

There was no uncooked food on the premises and the troops did not know when they would get any for us, so we were told that we had better made the Bakerite stew last for two days. Henningsen undertook to distribute it. I was glad to get out of the kitchen because it was now so full of smoke that it was impossible to see across it and Freddy Bridges and his crew looked like imps from hell as they worked in front of their stoves trying to coax them into heat.

I went off to see about blankets. The Japanese said they had two per man. In fact there were not even enough to issue one apiece.

After all this, another walk round with Henningsen to all thirty rooms to see how people were settling down. They couldn't be comfortable we knew, but a word or two on such an occasion can be very useful. I got back to room 14 at about nine o'clock and found that Murray had been able to save a bowl of stew which, though cold and congealed, was most welcome.

I had nearly finished eating when I was again sent for by Honda. Henningsen was already there. We had only a faint hope this time that Banjo had come up to scratch. It was only to receive orders for lights out and for morning roll call. Then to bed.

Bed wasn't very successful. Murray and I had three blankets between us, so we decided to bunk together, putting two on the floor and one plus two overcoats on top. Tired as I was the floor was terribly hard. It had been drizzling during the evening and towards midnight it started to pour. We might as well have had no roof for the amount of water that came in. Fortunately the floor sloped badly from the inside wall towards the outer one. There were some two inches of water against the far wall. We had to squeeze up on my side to make room for the unfortunates who had chosen places under the windows. It had been a long day, but the night seemed even longer.

12

FELLOW INMATES

THE second day in Haiphong Road dawned cold and wet. I found a wash-room and started off with a shave in icy water and a cold shower. There were not many shaves that day, but personally I was not going to appear in front of the Japanese looking as dejected as I felt. Breakfast was boiled rice and smoky tea. The stoves were in a terrible condition and quite unfit for regular cooking.

It soon became evident that the Japanese had made virtually no preparation for our reception. The place was filthy and there were no cleaning materials or stores of any description. The only food on hand was a couple of bags of rice and a box of tea of the poorest quality. There was a little coal but no firewood and we doubted our ability to start a coal fire with wet straw.

The buildings had originally been built for Chinese, probably some wealthy family. The old building, which we occupied, was typically Chinese in design. It had outer brick walls and tiled roof but the interior was mainly in wood. It consisted of two courtyards with two storeys of rooms on all four sides. The side common to both courtyards had a large hall on the ground floor through which communication between the two courtyards was maintained. The front of the building had three storeys with a large hall on the ground floor and good sized rooms in the wings. The top floor consisted of three communicating attic rooms, approached by a single narrow wooden stairway. It was popular principally because it boasted an open verandah from which it was possible to catch a glimpse of a few yards of Haiphong Road. The wives outside soon found this out. The whole building was very badly served with stairways and with the crowd of men we had, this might well have proved a death trap if we had been unlucky enought to have a fire.

The building occupied by the Japanese was far more desirable in every respect. It was a little smaller than our building but it never housed more than twenty Japanese as compared with our three hundred and sixty. There was also a low two-storeyed

PLAN OF HAIPHONG ROAD CAMP

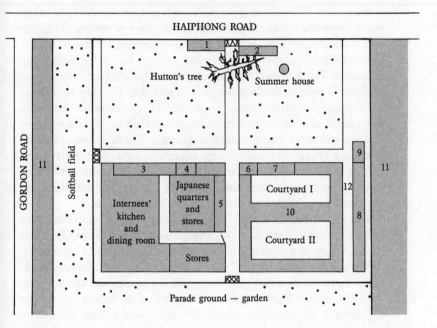

HAIPHONG ROAD

GORDON ROAD

1

2

Hutton's tree

Summer house

11

Softball field

3

4

5

Internees' kitchen and dining room

Japanese quarters and stores

Stores

6 7

Courtyard I

10

Courtyard II

9

12

8

11

Parade ground — garden

Key:

1 Guard room
2 Japanese kitchen
3 Japanese administrative build-ings
4 Colonel Odera's office
5 Japanese stores
6 Hugh Collar's office
7 Dr Sturton's clinic
8 Toilets and shower block
9 Garage
10 Internees' living quarters
11 Chinese houses

12 Traitors' alley — where collaborators in the camp exercised whilst the rest of the internees walked round the boundary wall

  Gates

Garden

Buildings

———— 12ft. high boundary wall

concrete building which contained the wash, shower and toilet rooms, furnace room, and a number of store rooms. Thanks to the fact that these premises had been leased fairly recently to the Fourth United State Marine Corps, we found ourselves very well provided with washing and toilet facilities.

There were a host of things to do during those first few days in camp. Food was going to be the most important, then as always. This was Henningsen's province. He had been working with it most of his life in one form or another and was obviously the one to get something organized. The fact that the Japanese were so little prepared for us was probably a blessing in disguise. At any rate they fell very readily for his suggestion that he should be allowed to telephone the American Association and ask them to send in cooked food to us until we were able to organize our own cooking arrangements. The first meal, consisting of sausage sandwiches, came in that afternoon, a very fine effort on the part of those outside, and particularly welcome since the stew which we were supposed to eat at midday had by then turned sour. Later on we would have eaten it and liked it, but not at that time.

Beds were asked for on that vital telephone call and camp beds were borrowed from the stores of the Shanghai Volunteer Corps. This was the beginning of a regular procession of trucks bringing in equipment, supplies and personal baggage. A receipt had to be signed for each truck-load. We insisted on this procedure, and if a receipt was not brought, we made one out. This was important because on the back of each receipt we wrote a list of requirements. We were very seldom allowed to telephone and this was for a long time our best means of communication.

By the end of this day we had an embryonic organization working. An office had been allotted to us. This had meant turning out the men who had spent the preceding night there. We had co-opted a number of assistants. There was far too much running about for two pairs of legs. I had picked on: W. J. Monk, former Chairman of the Shanghai Club, whom I valued for the weight he would carry; Harold Aiers, former Assistant to the Chief of Police who had worked for me before and who was particularly valuable for his help with the large police contingent; Henningsen and Bishop Ralph Ward, for weight; and as running dogs Arnhold Kiehn and Russel Brines. Brines was an A.P. free-lance correspondent who had spent some years in Japan and had picked up quite a bit of the language.

We had only one medical man, Dr T. B. Dunn, who started to organize medical services, ably assisted by Chief Pharmacist's Mate 'Doc'

Craddock who was one of the nicest men you could meet. There was also Ronnie Hillman who had some years of experience as a male nurse in a mental ward, and no training could have been more appropriate! I had located a master carpenter in Frankie Cook, whilst Eric Davies, President of the Boilermakers' Union on the outside, had volunteered to take charge of all engineering work.

More men arrived during the day, among them Bill Wright, later to share the job of camp representative with me, and Jimmy Forbes of my own company, ICI, who became camp cashier. Men continued to come in for about a week, among the last comers being Dr Stephen D. Sturton and Bishop Curtis. These two had been arrested in Hangchow and brought down to Shanghai. Sturton later received the OBE for the sterling work that he had done as Medical Superintendent of a Mission Hospital in Hangchow where he had treated hundreds of wounded Chinese soldiers. This was probably why the Japanese had picked on him. If I say that the Bishop was Irish, with all the courage of his Irish convictions, that is probably a quite adequate explanation for the dislike that the Japanese had taken to him.

When the round-up was completed, we had about three hundred and sixty men in all in the Haiphong Road Camp. They consisted of approximately two hundred and seventy British, sixty Americans, twenty Dutch, fourteen Greeks, one Norwegian and one Belgian. They proved to be as complete a cross section of humanity as one could hope to see. Every kind from Taipans to beachcombers, they ranged in age from twenty to seventy-two. We never did find out how the selection had been made. Were we political prisoners? Were we selected as hostages? Had we been picked at random out of the telephone book? None of these explanations quite filled the bill.

The Greeks were a curious mixture. More than half of them were sailors who had been stranded in Shanghai on the outbreak of war. In no sense could they be regarded as political offenders and it is my own opinion that they were put in as a lesson to the rest of them who had created a disturbance at the Japanese Consulate in protest at the handling of Greek relief. All of them were memorable, for their virtues or their vices, or for both. There was Kaplanides — 'Cappy', Second Engineer, a first class mechanic and a hard and willing worker, probably the most genuinely popular of them all. Neofitos, the real strong man of the party, could drive a six-inch nail through a two-inch plank with one blow of his fist and then pull it out with his teeth. Although he had a fierce temper, it was fortunate that he never let himself go in the many disputes that racked our Greek community. The Gendarmerie had him out from questioning three times, only for brief periods, but they put him through it pretty thoroughly. He took it very calmly and appeared to bear no grudge, but I am sure they got nothing out of him. Arapoglu was the 'phoney' strong man. For the first year he did physical exercises about six hours a day, yet all but mutinied when called upon to work, and we were all a little frightened of him. He put up a good bluff. He turned out to be just simple minded, and became almost tractable. He gave me one of the biggest surprises I had in camp one day by asking me in very broken English whether I thought honesty of purpose was more important than the acquisition of knowledge. I had never credited him with two connected thoughts, let alone an interest in philosophical discussion. Papagborgiou, 'Papa', was a red-hot communist, with a badly set and permanently bent right arm, which did not prevent him from learning to pitch a good horseshoe, or from playing an unskilled but very amusing game of softball. Ginger Arvanitis, as hot tempered as his hair, was the only man whom I ever threatened to throw out of the office if he did not keep a civil tongue in his head.

The remaining Greeks were business men. One was the epitome of arrogance and superiority and was never able to stomach the fact that he did not receive preferential treatment over his less fortunate countrymen.

The two groups were constantly at loggerheads, with those in the centre frequently shifting to left or right so that there was never any stability in the balance of power. They gave me more headaches than all the rest of the camp put together, but I should still be glad to meet most of them again — definitely only one at a time.

The one Norwegian, by passport, had been born a Russian Jew, Jacob Shriro. Few men in the camp will forget that name. He had made money, big money, and was an industrialist of note in Shanghai. When the exodus of Jews from Central Europe started, China was one of the few countries that was open to them. No Chinese visa was needed for entry into Shanghai, and to Shanghai they came in their tens of thousands. They became an immediate relief problem and Shriro contributed very largely indeed out of his personal fortune. But he was a particularly fair-minded man. He decided that it was not right that he should give only to his own people, for had he not made his money equally from the Gentiles? So he contributed substantial sums to the various churches and missions in Shanghai, including the Church of England, and to Chinese charities. His fairmindedness was his undoing. Among the recipients of his generosity was the American Methodist Church, of which Bishop Ralph Ward was the head. The Japanese believed that the Methodist Church and its affiliated mission had collected information of a military nature for the benefit of the American Forces. So Bishop Ward was gathered into the fold at Haiphong Road, and in due course was escorted out of the gates by the Gendarmerie and submitted to gentle questioning, so gentle that he was in hospital for much of the remainder of his period of internment. Later on, Shriro was questioned on the same subject, but this was carried out at night within the confines of the camp. I did not learn until afterwards that he had had a tooth knocked out during his interrogation. He did not tell me because he did not want to add to my worries. Shriro's associates on the outside had access to funds, and we devised means whereby he could communicate with them. No man in camp ever appealed in vain to Shriro for financial help.

Pierard, the first Belgian inmate, came to us from Bridge House. He had been one of a mixed party which had tried to escape overland to Chunking. They had been delayed for some reason in the neighbourhood of the Ta Hu Lakes and a Chinese messenger had been despatched to Shanghai for supplies. He had been caught at the railway barrier on Hungjao Road, tortured and finally forced to reveal the location of the party. They were caught, brought back to Shanghai, and put into Bridge House. Among them was Corinne Bernfeldt, who later committed suicide. Pierard had taken the line that he was a Belgian subject, technically not at war with Japan, and there was no law prohibiting him from taking a walk in the country if he wished. This did not dissuade the Japanese from keeping him in Bridge House for nearly four months.

We had known collaborators in the camp with us from the start. In the confusion of the first night they had all found space somewhere, and once they were in we were able to keep them where they had planted themselves.

My problem was that no-one wanted to share with them, and we had no cells or single rooms in which to put them. The guards would not permit people to sleep in corridors and at times I had to move a collaborator around each night until he left the camp. Some left to continue their work, but some chose to stay, despite the constant ostracism.

These men were of differing nationalities and presumably had their own personal reasons for siding with the Japanese. Some were ignorant, misguided people who had fallen on hard times. One could not sympathize with them, but perhaps could understand. The other renegades were men with brains and education, and these one found it hard to tolerate. No one wanted to associate with them and although a room had to be shared with them, they ate alone, worked alone, and exercised alone. At one time the cooks refused to cater for them, and I had to take the stand that all internees must be treated alike, irrespective of personal feelings. Once an exception was made to that rule, there would have been chaos in the camp organization.

On the whole I had the highest regard for the honesty and purpose of most of the personalities in camp. The constant trouble-makers represented only a very small proportion of the total. The circumstances were peculiarly trying, the monotony of the daily routine, no change of faces, no change of surroundings, the constant indignity of being compelled to take orders from the Japanese, the lack of world news, the absurd and unreasonable instructions, caused one to live in a constant state of mixed exasperation and futility. Believe me, if you wanted to find out who were the men on whom you could rely, being a prisoner in Shanghai was the way to find out.

13
KEEPING OCCUPIED

WE realized from the start that the only way to keep men sane and moderately happy was to keep them as fully employed as possible. A day or two after the camp was set up, Henningsen and I were called across to see Honda and the Colonel. We were told that they wished the camp to be self-governing, and that we two were to set up the necessary organization, and to act as liaison between the men and our Japanese guardians. They would issue general instructions of a procedural nature only, which would be passed on to the men through us. It would be up to us to see that the orders were carried out. Any man who made trouble should be reported to them and they would deal with him.

By and large, this suited us very well. The less direct contact the men had with the Japanese, the less likelihood there would be of trouble. If orders were passed through us, we should have the opportunity of discussing them and if necessary of arguing over them with the Japanese, before obviously unsuitable ones were put into effect. This was particularly important in view of the difficulty in getting them to amend an order once it had been made public. Just what they meant by the camp being self-governing we could only find out by experience, but we meant to make it as close to self-government as possible. The net result was that we should probably save the Japanese a great deal of work and trouble — which was to be deplored, but the benefits on our side resulting from being freed from constant detailed supervision would be very great indeed. As regards the question of reporting delinquents to the Japanese, we decided very promptly that we could only regard this as the lowest form of indignity and that nothing short of dire emergency would make us do so. We never did. The only time that I was really tempted to break this resolution was in the case of a man whom we caught in the act of passing a note to the Japanese reporting an infraction of their rules.

Having received our instructions, we set about creating a permanent organization. It was not simply a question of creating an organization that would get the essential work of the camp done quickly and efficiently. That could be done with a fraction of the numbers at our disposal. It was rather a question of so arranging matters that every man in the camp who was not actually prostrated by illness should have some kind of job to do, and further, in some measure to organize for the leisure hours as well. We also had to try to spread the more responsible posts over the various nationalities, so that it could not be said that the camp was being run by the British, or by the Americans. We were all in the same boat and we felt that we should take every care to avoid anything which might foster unhealthy international feeling.

Under the circumstances neither Henningsen nor I was very much in favour of government by committee. We had been ordered to do a job which we did not much fancy, but if we had to do it, we would do it as far as possible in our own way. Consultation there must be. The camp must have an opportunity of stating its views, and we must have a means of keeping in touch with camp opinion, but since we could not dictate to the Japanese, we could not have a committee dictating to us. We could not ignore the wishes of the camp on purely internal matters, but we should have to be the judge on the extent to which matters of organization and procedure could safely be regarded as purely internal affairs in which the Japanese would take no interest.

We therefore set up a Captains' Committee. This was composed of all thirty-one room captains. Through it we could transmit the orders of the Japanese and the views of the camp could be ascertained and expressed. It met daily at first, latterly once weekly, or more often if the need arose to obtain an immediate decision on any particular point. Its functions were never very clearly defined, but on the whole it worked very well. It became in effect partly advisory and partly mandatory, as we became able, in the light of actual experience, to determine what kind of decision could be taken without reference to the Japanese. The Camp Representatives always retained the right to veto any particular decision of the committee, even on internal affairs, but in fact the veto was very seldom exercised.

In setting up the Committee, we realized that our earlier selection of Room Captains had not been made on the proper basis. It will be remembered that the Japanese had said that we should choose brawn rather than brains. We therefore arranged for elections to be held after the first week or two when we realized what characteristics were desirable, and had given the men in each room time to become acquainted

The Collars' home, 1933 – 1942, 17 Crescent Avenue, The ICI Compound, Shanghai.

Rowing on Soochow Creek in pre-war Shanghai. Hugh Collar is the Stroke.

The author (*second from right*) with other members of the Machine Gun Company, Shanghai Volunteer Corps.

Hugh Collar with his wife Bunty and daughters Deirdre (*left*) and Julie (*right*), 1940.

Refugees from outlying areas crowding into the International Settlement, Shanghai, August 1937.

Crowds of refugees throng the Bund and adjacent streets in Shanghai after Chinese airmen had bombed the downtown area, August 1937.

The author's registration armband. 'In a spirit of bravado, I chose to wear armband No. 1.'

Official photograph on the front steps of the Haiphong Road Camp. Front row: (*from left to right*) Hugh Collar, Anker B. Henningsen, Somekawa — the Japanese civilian interpreter, and Lt. 'Dogface' Miyazaki.

Camp representatives Anker B. Henningsen (*left*) and Hugh Collar (*right*) with Japanese officials at the Haiphong Road Camp. (*From left to right*) Lt. Honda, Colonel Odera, and Lt. 'Dogface' Miyazaki.

Hugh Collar and Anker B. Henningsen in the grounds of the Haiphong Road Camp. (*Above*) with Lt. Honda, and (*below*) outside their office.

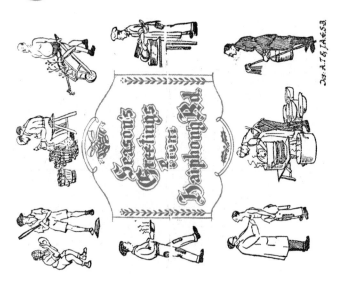

A Christmas card made at the camp, 1943.

and to size each other up. It was really surprising how few changes were made during the life of the camp, and when changes did occur, it was usually because the incumbent became fed up with the job and was unwilling to carry on. It entailed quite a lot of work and responsibility and inevitably brought with it much criticism from those in the room who did not approve of this or that action. Most of the Room Captains took this responsibility very seriously, and did their best to make the men whom they represented understand the reasons prompting various lines of action, and the difficulties which we faced *vis-à-vis* the Japanese.

Camp work was divided into two main classes, specialist and non-specialist. The former was in the main done by permanent groups of men, and the latter, being more monotonous, was done by casual labour under an arrangement which rotated the men through several jobs on which they worked for a week at a time. This latter group tended to diminish at the expense of the former. Men became accustomed to working together, and in order not to be split up by the varying needs of the labour pool, picked out a job and made it their own. In the end, the job of vegetable cleaning, which became almost non-existent anyway, because there were no vegetables, and the straight sweeping up jobs, became the only ones which were not done by permanent gangs. One would have thought that a job like drain cleaning would have been the last instead of the first to attract a permanent gang and yet it was one of the favourites. I believe that from the day a broom was first put into their hands, Basil Wallace and his faithful few swept drains and cleaned cesspools every single day, wet or fine, including Sundays, for just under three solid years, an unattractive but very vital job — one of the few jobs that had no perquisites. Wallace must have possessed a supreme sense of duty. Fengtai, our home for the last two months of the war must have caused a frightful gap in his life.

The specialist groups were: the medical and sickroom staff under doctors Dunn and Sturton; the engineers, covering boiler maintenance, plumbing, and electrical work under Eric Davies; the carpenters under Frank Cook; and the cooks under R.A. Kreulen, who had been head of the Netherlands Relief Committee. The labour pool for sundry jobs was looked after by Road, an American, and Sam Tweedie, British.

On the recreational side, it was clear that organized games alone would be nothing like sufficient. Our facilities were greatly limited both in equipment and space, and we should have to anticipate long periods of bad weather when outdoor games would be out of the question. It appeared probable that educational courses would prove interesting and a quick canvas revealed that we had several trained teachers and a number of other men who were sufficiently expert to give lessons. A.E. Thornton, who had been Principal of the Lester Technical Institute, took charge of the educational activities, which proved remarkably popular. There were classes in elementary and advanced English, French, Spanish, German, Russian, Chinese in the Mandarin, Canton, and Shanghai dialects, mathematics, navigation (described I think as terrestrial mathematics for the benefit of the Japanese). There was a veterinary class, shorthand, book-keeping, engineering, domestic plumbing and repairs, and First Aid. In addition to these open classes there was much private tuition in subjects for which there was not a wide demand. Many men left the camp far better fitted to earn a living in a competitive world than when they entered it. The classes were really valuable, not merely for their educational benefit, but rather for the time they occupied, the interest they added, and the resulting enormous benefit to morale.

On the lighter side, we had a really first-class organizer of dramatics in E.G. Smith-Wright. Some of the shows were really magnificent, the setting and effects quite incredible.

In due course we created an orchestra. The big drum was an empty barrel with canvas stretched over the end. The wind instruments were lent by the Prisoners of War Camp from their Marine Band surplus. The double bass was made in the camp as were guitars, ukeleles, and various other stringed instruments. I haven't a trained ear, but that band sounded really good to me.

Lectures were also arranged. These were on subjects of general interest and took place usually in the evenings after supper. They were more difficult to work up, partly because men were rather diffident about standing up in front of the whole camp and saying their piece, but more particularly because the Japanese insisted that the lecture be submitted to them in duplicate beforehand for their approval. This meant that the lecturer could not speak from brief notes but had to write the whole thing out longhand and then have it typed. Then it went to Honda who took his duties very conscientiously and would take anything up to three weeks or a month going through it word for word with the aid of a small Japanese/English dictionary.

It must not be supposed that this organization was created in a day. The essentials went into action very quickly, but the whole picture took a considerable time to round out. When it was in full working order, no man needed to find time hanging heavily on his hands. The specialists and men with responsible jobs had no worries in this direction. Their difficulty was rather to find the time in which to do all that they wanted. In my own case there were many classes which I should have liked to attend but I simply didn't have time. The man with a small job in the labour pool on the other hand might find his work for the day finished by 10 a.m. He could then attend classes from 10 until lunch, with some running also into the afternoon. Sports, as a spectator or participant, might occupy his time until supper time. After that there were card games, chess, reading, or occasional special shows to pass the time until lights out. In the intervals, there were always jobs of personal laundry, mending, repairs, scrounging and so on to keep them occupied.

One of our big difficulties was lack of equipment. When we entered the building, it was not much more than an empty shell. Lt. Honda told us himself later on that he had not been told until the night before our arrest that he was to be in charge of our camp, and he had not even seen the place until the morning of our arrival. He had no idea of the material requirements of a camp such as this, and would not have had time to get them if he had. He was completely overwhelmed by the list of requirements that we put in front of him. Most of them he simply rejected out of hand with the statement that the Japanese Army did not supply this kind of thing. With others it was, 'maybe we can get this, but I think take long time'. We had to decide very early on whether we would, as a matter of principle, do as little as possible towards equipping and maintaining the camp, leaving everything to the Japanese; or whether we should obtain for ourselves all the equipment we considered necessary in order to make the place habitable and keep it in good repair, and trust to being able to recover the cost from the Japanese after the war. The Association had already offered to act as our suppliers and to finance any purchases which might be necessary. Much could probably be borrowed.

Some things brooked no delay: medicines, medical equipment, and sick room supplies we must have immediately. Nearly all the toilets needed fixing. The Japanese had used a country type outhouse accommodating four men which was totally inadequate for our three hundred and sixty. It was too expensive to go on getting food sent in from the American School and we must get equipment in readiness for the day when we must start cooking for ourselves. There was no fire fighting equipment. We would have been delighted to see the place burn down but there would inevitably have been some of our own men inside.

It was soon evident that we simply had to go ahead and consider ourselves lucky that they did not object to our getting these things for ourselves. This is not so absurd as it sounds. Permitting us to bring in supplies was a tacit admission that they were unable to do so. This might involve loss of face, if badly handled. If it had been left to Honda I am sure that he would have refused permission had he not been overruled by Colonel Odera. The latter was CO first of the Prisoners of War Camp, and now of us: he had a very nice cushy job. He did not want anything to disturb the serenity of his existence and he realized that he would have a much better time if his charges were relatively comfortable, and if that comfort could be achieved at no cost to the Japanese Government, it was a perfectly splendid arrangement.

So we were allowed to look after ourselves. We found in the end that we had to get practically everything, even down to cleaning materials. There were men in the camp who did not approve of our policy of ordering our requirements from the outside, but they were very much in the minority. We had one awkward moment. The Associations had been in the habit of submitting periodic financial statements to the Swiss Consulate and this became obligatory when they started to draw on their home Governments for funds. After some months an item of some Chinese dollars 180,000, representing the cost of supplies to the Haiphong Road Camp, appeared in the accounts of the British Residents' Association and was duly cabled to England by the Swiss. A protest and request for explanation was forwarded to the Japanese Foreign Office through the Swiss Embassy in Tokyo. This produced a request for explanation to Colonel Odera who promptly called in Henningsen and myself for a royal dressing down. Here he had been doing everything possible to help us and the only result of his very generous treatment was a protest from the British Government.

It was difficult. The protest was undoubtedly justified. The Japanese failure to provide adequate equipment was simply scandalous. However, we were most anxious that the Colonel should not clamp down on future supplies. We simply had to have them and if the Japanese would not give them to us we had to maintain the existing avenues by which they came in from outside. The old boy was really very upset indeed. He was obviously trembling for his job. We certainly did not want a change. His laziness and inefficiency was our safeguard so he just had to be whitewashed somehow.

We finally placated him by submitting memorandum giving the principal headings of expenditure and stating that these were in the main ordered to meet western standards of comfort which called for equipment and materials which an army in the field could not be expected to supply. We further expressed our appreciation of the co-operation which the camp authorities had shown in enabling us to obtain our equipment requirements. It hurt, but it was undoubtedly politic, and as soon as we could, we let the Association know of our difficulty and how we had met it, and asked them to let the British Foreign Office know the true picture. The US Government, taking a more realistic view, did not protest.

I had three years of almost daily arguments with Lt. Honda, which usually made me want to vomit. In expendables, they gave us food and fuel in steadily diminishing quantities, and occasional issues of toilet soap and toilet paper. Of medicines, all that they provided were cholera injections and smallpox vaccines, and on one occasion, anti-dysentery injections. The latter was used over the heated protests of doctors Dunn and Sturton who favoured pouring it down the drain and removing the Japanese outhouse as being more likely to be of prophylactic value. It was a tremendous argument, typically Honda. Here was this man, whose pre-war vocation was the export of cheap Japanese pottery and toys, laying down the law on medical matters to two highly skilled medicos. His utter lack of modesty was quite incredible.

14

FOOD PROBLEMS

WITH a full belly, one can face the world with some measure of confidence; without it, nothing else is of any consequence at all. Not that we ever starved, or even came really near to it, but we were hungry for long periods.

It was some time before we knew what our official food rations would be, and with meals coming in from the American school we had not had cause to worry much about it. We were in any case lacking the equipment in which to cook it. The Colonel then called us into consultation and produced his figures giving the official ration issue. This consisted of stated daily quantities of rice or bread, meat or fish, sugar, sauce, salt and vegetables. They were not high, but seemed not unreasonable, particularly if we could supplement them. The vegetable figure was somewhat vague, being based on a budgetary allowance, not on weight. Only experience would show what could be bought with the allowance. Rising prices were to prove it hopelessly inadequate.

At about this time we were advised that our Governments would make us monthly allowances of 'Comfort Money' at the official rate for Prisoners of War of £2 per month or US$8, all, that is, except the Greeks, whose government appeared to be a bit slow in coming to the aid of its nationals. This money was made available to us through the Swiss Consulate in local dollars at the prevailing open market rate of exchange. Although the allowance was really intended to enable prisoners to purchase small luxuries such as cigarettes and toilet articles, it was clear that we should have to spend the major part of it on food. It was also evident that the money would be most wisely and economically spent on buying bulk stores for use in the kitchen, and also with a view to laying in a reserve supply for the future.

It was not a straightforward problem. The allowances were made to the individual internees, and there were naturally a number of men who claimed their right to dispose of their money as they thought fit. We had a number of debates on the principle involved, which was whether or not in matters of this kind the camp should be governed by the vote of the majority. The largest body of objectors were men who had families or dependents living in the town who were badly in need of help, some of whom did not even qualify for relief payments from the Swiss Consulate. These men naturally wanted to send their comfort allowance out to their dependents. I was able to help the most urgent of these British cases through the generosity of fellow internees, Mr J. H. Green, Far Eastern Manager of Thomas Cook and Sons, in conjunction with Mr J. Shriro.

The centralized buying of food supplies was organized by a finance and a dietary committee. The dietary committee was composed of our resident doctors who recommended the nature and quantities of food to be bought to give a balanced diet. Meanwhile the finance committee made a monthly review of the stock and monetary position and would submit their recommendations through the camp office. Only part of the incoming funds were sequestered for the centralized buying of food, and as much as possible was left for the individual to spend as he wished. This system was followed as long as Comfort Allowances were coming into the camp and worked very smoothly and well. I do not think that any of the other camps adopted this method, and as a result, our kitchen probably produced a more plentiful and more balanced diet than any of the others, although our basic ration from the Japanese was much smaller.

The scheme first proved its value in the spring of 1944 when 'Comfort Money' stopped for three months. The Swiss Consulate had been selling Swiss Francs at the best rate on the open Shanghai market in order to provide us with local dollars. As the local dollar depreciated in value, we received more and more of them for the same number of Swiss Francs, and had been able to keep abreast of rising prices. The Japanese suddenly instructed the Consulate that in future they must sell their Swiss Francs only to the Yokohama Specie Bank, and at the official pre-war rates of exchange. They were no doubt theoretically within their rights, but it was a most unrealistic viewpoint. It would have meant that each internee would receive only about thirty dollars a month, the price of fifty cigarettes, instead of the thousand or so dollars which we were then getting. Our Governments very properly objected, but the Japanese were obdurate. They knew that they had only to sit back until we really began to starve, when our Governments would have to give way. They only had to wait three months. In the meantime, we had been able to get by without undue hardship by drawing on the reserves which we had created out of our centralized buying.

The payment of Comfort Allowances was resumed but at a very high cost to the Home Governments. As prices continued to rise, the local dollar allowance had to be increased until we were getting about sixteen hundred dollars a month each, and needed much more. This was costing the British Government one hundred pounds per man per month, and the total cost of internees and their dependents in Shanghai must have been nearly one million pounds per month, which was a virtual gift to the Japanese. At this point, the Home Governments struck together, and this time there was virtually no hope of a resumption. We would have to fend for ourselves. The Japanese daily ration was down to five ounces of bread (some days we had none), one bowl of rice, half an ounce of raw meat or fish, and a negligible quantity of fresh vegetables. Prices were rising to astronomic levels in local dollars, and supplies were becoming very scarce. We could see the time coming when local farmers and other suppliers would refuse to accept paper dollars at all and would only trade on a barter basis. This would be impossible for us to negotiate and we felt that we must make every effort to buy supplies as far forward as we could whilst money still had some value.

It was clear that we could do nothing without outside help, and without some intermediary inside the camp who would act as go-between. Shriro once again came to the rescue as far as the provision of funds was concerned. He was quite willing to advance the local dollars against promise of payment after the war in US dollars, provided that his contacts in Shanghai could raise the necessary figure, and could apply it without risk of it being traced back to them. The intermediary within the camp was T. Somekawa, our civilian Japanese interpreter. He was a man of sixty or so, who had spent many years in the States, and had always proved himself sympathetic and reasonable in his attitude towards us. He agreed to carry our messages to those concerned on the outside.

The scheme was that the goods should be supplied to the International Red Cross, and that they should send them to the camp as an anonymous donation. Since their own funds were under rigid inspection and some measure of control by the Japanese, we could not simply have the cash handed over to them without the risk of sources being betrayed. The whole scheme went through as planned, and in this way we got in about six months' supply of wheat, lima beans and lard, our main supplements to the Japanese rations. No more than six people in the camp knew that it was anything other than what it purported to be. We would have preferred to let everyone know, so that they could appreciate their debt to Jack Liddell, who acted as guarantor to Shriro, but the risks of the Japanese getting to know were altogether too great.

Shortly after the camp was set up, the Colonel appointed two official suppliers. The first, who bought our bulk supplies, gave us extremely good service, and his prices were even well below those quoted by the Red Cross. Later on we discovered how it was that we fared so well. The process as far as we could gather was this. We would give our order, which had then to be countersigned and approved by the Japanese Quartermaster. He would treat them as part of the official Japanese rations for the camp, which meant that army trucks could be used for their transport. The order would also be increased several fold. Armed with the requisite documents, and with free transport provided, our supplier would depart for the country and buy the goods, which were duly brought back to town and deposited on his store. Our portion would then be brought to us on handcarts and the remainder sold on the local market. Since he had no transport charges to pay, and had also avoided all the usual taxation and squeeze paid by any Chinese trader, he could sell at prices bringing him in a very large profit. He was a sufficiently good business man to let us have our modest share at a very moderate rate of profit in order to keep us buying, for should our buying cease so would his opportunity for these very profitable large scale transactions. I do not know how many ways the profit was split. The Quartermaster almost certainly took the lion's share, but Lt. Honda's salary was only one hundred yen a month, which did not prevent him from spending a great deal of money on expensive cameras.

Our food problem was not one of quantity alone. Cooking itself became increasingly difficult as supplies of fuel were progressively reduced. For the best part of the last year, we were down to two tons of coal per month and a small and uncertain amount of kindling. The coal was mainly dust and had to be converted into briquettes to be useable. The local mud had no binding qualities and we did a lot of experimenting before finding the best formula. We used mainly a starch made from flour and rice. It went against the grain to have to use part of our precious food supplies to make briquettes but we could not cook without them. Another binder which we used when we had it was our irregular and variable issue of extremely coarse toilet paper.

As coal supplies were reduced, we had to simplify our cooking arrangements. All our beautiful American stoves had to be abandoned, and we came down to four boiling pans set in brickwork, each holding about twenty gallons. We had neither the coal nor the kindling to permit lighting of the stoves more than once a day so we had to run the day's cooking straight through. As soon as the breakfast of cracked wheat porridge was cooked, the lunch-time stew and rice went on. That would be cooked by about eleven o'clock when it was ladled out and as much as possible put into an enormous hay box which we constructed out of bits and pieces. The evening rice then went into the pans. By the time that was cooked, it was lunch time. The contents of the hay box container were eaten, it was cleaned, and the evening meal went in. The stoves were then let out for the day. That is how it went, day in, day out, porridge, stew, rice or beans. Not very appetising but fairly filling and on the whole quite nourishing. Nobody got fat, but on the other hand nobody had to starve provided that they could get it down.

There were times when it was pretty difficult to get some of it down, particularly the rice. This was of very variable quality, varying from poor to stinking. Supplies usually came in every five days or so. We would be issued with the exact ration for the next five days. Occasionally there would be a delay of a day or two because the trucks had broken down, or had used up their fuel allowance, or the store was closed when they arrived or some equally futile excuse. I tried many times to persuade the Quartermaster to bring in a reserve to provide for such delays, but without success until one day when both trucks went out and came back bringing two months' supplies, and marvel of marvels, none of it went into the Quartermaster's store at the back of the kitchen. The gang started to unload. I had a hurried call from the storekeeper. Would I come and look at the new rice? It was hot. Some of it was so hot that it was painful to shove a fist down inside the sack. It was immediately clear that the consignment had in some way been pushed on to us to get rid of it in a hurry.

I went for Honda on the run and made him examine it. He knew perfectly well that a swift one was being put over on us by the Quartermaster but had not the guts to make him return it to the store. All that he would say was that it was 'perfect', in spite of the very strongest remonstrances from our dietary committee. He knew perfectly well that he was in the wrong and had not a leg to stand on, and I was able to tell him exactly what I thought of him and the Quartermaster in most unparliamentary language without provoking the smallest comeback.

The stuff was beginning to steam and stink and had we left it as it was it would have rotted away completely in a few days. All that we could do was to clear all tables and benches out of the messroom, empty all the sacks on to the concrete floor, keep it constantly turned, and give it a chance to cool off and dry out. That was a bad two months. Many of the men could not take it at all. Only the very strongest stomachs, such as mine, could hold it down.

Breakfast would have been a good meal, if we had always had enough of it. Very plain, but like all good plain foods, not unbearably monotonous. We first learnt the value of cracked wheat from the supplies turned over to us by the American Red Cross. We found it so good, both from the nutritional and medical viewpoints, and also because it was so much more palatable than the rice or congee, which formed the breakfast meal in most of the other camps, that we determined to try it for ourselves.

It took us a long time to perfect our process but in the end it was something to be proud of. Our raw wheat was bought from the country through our Japanese supplier and came straight from the threshing floor. A Chinese threshing floor is simply a circle of packed mud, and the wheat grains are swept up, together with such dust and grit as inevitably, or intentionally, becomes mixed with it. We devised a wheat-washing machine which came close to perfection. Once washed, the whole grain was spread out to dry, and then given a final drying in the cooking pans. This gave the wheat a very pleasant nutty flavour, and made it crack more easily in our stone mills.

The cracking or grinding was done in two ordinary Chinese stone mills, consisting of one circular stone superimposed on another, the top one being rotated by hand, whilst the grain was fed in through a hole in the centre. Even this simple sounding job became an expert chore. When we first tried it out we estimated that it would take us eight hours to grind enough for the daily meal and that we should need a gang of twelve men, taking turn and turn about. We got it down to about two hours with two men doing the whole job.

Garlic was one of the cook's most important materials. Our meat was usually slaughterhouse scraps, compressed into blocks and frozen. It was frequently exceedingly high but we had so little that we could not afford to throw it away unless it was actually crawling. That was where the garlic came in. One could always judge the quality of the meat by the amount of garlic that the cooks had to put in to cover the taint. We could not see the meat. With the small quantity we had, it was found best to grind it in the mincer. This got the flavour through the whole of the stew and removed all risk of charges of favouritism in its distribution.

15

CONTINUING TRAGEDY

FOR the first two years the camp was under surveillance by the Gendarmerie and for a time it appeared as though they had placed in the camp all the men whom they felt that they would like to question. As far as we could make out, all men who were taken into Bridge House from the outside were sent to us on release. They were very sorry specimens by the time they came to us.

We developed a definite technique for dealing with them: barber, bath, a light meal, plenty of hot drinks, and then to bed in our camp hospital. Their next need was to talk. They had all of course been warned against talking of what had happened to them within the confines of Bridge House, but they had been so repressed, and their relief at getting out was so great, that they simply had to be allowed to work off steam somehow. We knew that there were stool-pigeons in the camp, mainly rather weaker vessels who had themselves been through the mill of Bridge House and had agreed to act as spies for the Gendarmerie under threats of one kind and another. We thought that we knew all of them but could never be quite sure. We therefore allowed the newcomers a very few carefully selected visitors to whom they could safely talk and say all they wanted. We kept them in the hospital until Dr Sturton judged that the strain had worked off sufficiently for it to be safe to allow them to mix again with the general public without fear that the desire to talk unwisely would get the better of them.

One day we had a consignment of eight. This included A.V.T. Dean, Revd W.H. Hudspeth, W.S. Bungey, G.H. Forrestier, K.W. Johnstone and W.N. Dickson. All were seriously emaciated, with long hair and beards and had been through it pretty badly. Most, if not all, had undergone the whole procedure up to and including the water cure. Dean had it several times without their getting anything out of him. They had jumped on Bungey so hard that the pressure of water had burst both eardrums so that they were badly septic. One can never forget the sight of those men, and their pathetic gratitude for the least little act of service or kindness. I think that this, more even than the dreadful tales that they had to tell, made one realize something of what they had been through. I remember too how Dean could not bear at first to part with his beautiful silky grey beard and how he would sit on his bed quietly stroking it between his fingers for hours at a time.

There was also a steady stream of men being taken out of the camp to Bridge House by the camp Gendarmes, whilst a large number were also put through interrogation inside the camp itself. It began to look as though the whole of the camp was going to get a turn, which did not in the least add to our peace of mind, particularly those of us who expected to find ourselves fairly high up on the list and could think of a number of subjects on which we should not like to be pressed too hard. The procedure was usually for Honda to send for me, and tell me to call so and so to the office, with the added phrase:

'Tell him to put his overcoat on.'

There would be a rapid scurry by the men in his room to fill his pockets with biscuits, cigarettes and toilet paper and then we would stand outside the office watching another unfortunate being led away, wondering how he would take it and who would be next.

This went on for many months and culminated in the Hutton case. This was different from the others, apart from its tragic outcome, in that the questioning arose from the alleged commission of an offence within the camp.

It started on a summer evening. I was sitting in the office when I heard the muffled growling of many voices outside my window, which told a tale of angry men. It sounded like trouble for me, and I went outside to see what particular form the latest headache was taking. I was just in time to see one of the Sikh guards, a particularly revolting cross-eyed specimen, Amar Singh by name, dragging J. M. Watson up the steps into Honda's office. It was not long before Honda sent for me and I found him with Watson, the Sikh guard, and our two Gendarmes in a state of high excitement. He said that Watson had tried to persuade the Sikh to smuggle a message out of the camp for him, concealed in a hollowed out pencil. Honda unfortunately had the pencil which definitely put Watson on the spot. The message was fortunately quite innocuous, but the Sikh said that there was another man involved with Watson, and Honda wanted to know who it was. He was also threatening all sorts of dire penalties against the camp as a whole, regarding this thing as a very poor return for his many kindnesses to us. He ordered an instant parade of all men in their rooms in order that the second culprit might be identified. The fall-in was blown and at the parade which followed, R.H. Ekin, a room-mate of Watson, was picked out as the other culprit. Both Watson and Ekin were submitted to a lengthy interrogation lasting late into the night, and assisted by a liberal use of bamboo fencing swords.

In the morning, Honda ordered me to send Watson and Ekin to him and to tell them that they would be taken out by the Gendarmes for punishment. I went into the office to ask Harold Aiers to fetch one of them whilst I called the other. He then told me that Ekin had been wrongly identified at the parade of the previous evening and that Hutton had been the man with Watson when he accosted the Sikh guard. I felt pretty sure that Hutton would not want anyone else to take the rap for him, and it would in any case be only fair to tell him the latest development. As soon as I told him, Hutton asked me to tell Honda that a mistake had been made and that it was he, not Ekin, who had been talking with Watson. That is how it came about that Hutton went out to his death, voluntarily, in order that another should not suffer in his place.

We often thought of calling the big plane tree in the yard 'Hutton's tree'. About ten days after he and Watson were taken out, a summer typhoon of more than usual violence hit Shanghai. We were flooded inside and out, and during the night the big plane tree which stood by the side of the main avenue, in front of the Japanese office and which gave much welcome shade in summer, was blown down. It fell right across the road, blocking the entrance for all but small cars. Our own lorries could not go in or out to collect food supplies and we decided that it would be best to cut the tree up as it lay. We were about to start when the Colonel arrived and insisted that we should try to re-erect it and save it. Although he proved to be right, we were very dubious about the feasibility of the suggestion. We should need all hands on the job, and we had some difficulty in getting the men together since they were busy trying to dry out their gear that had been soaked in the storm.

We had lopped off the top, and with about a hundred men tailing on a rope on one side, and shoving on beams on the other, had just raised the tree to an angle of about thirty degrees, when a black sedan came through the gate. It could not pass us, but turned left down a narrow pathway and pulled up in front of our clinic. Most of us working on the tree hardly noticed it. A few minutes later, Steve Mills came running across to me and told me that the car had just brought back Hutton and Watson and that I simply must come and see the condition they were in.

The tree raising had just reached a critical point and I had seen too many men come back from the hands of the Gendarmerie to think that this would be anything that I had not seen before. I therefore did not turn away immediately, but within seconds the matter was taken out of my hands. Other men had come across with Mills and spread the news. So many men stopped work that the tree immediately fell down again. The Colonel shouted to know why the work had stopped and ordered us to get back on the job but nobody paid the least attention to him.

By the time I reached the clinic, Hutton and Watson had been taken out of the car and were inside. Watson was in fair shape, that is he could talk and walk, but Hutton had been lying unconscious on the floor of the car and had to be carried in. I found him lying on a stretcher on the floor of the clinic, completely naked. His wrists and ankles were badly lacerated, showing clearly that he had been tightly bound, and he was indescribably filthy. He had left camp a strong, well-built man of somewhat above average size, and had returned a barely living skeleton, all in the space of ten days or so. Doctors Dunn and Sturton were attending to him and after a brief examination told me that he was seriously dehydrated. I did not need to be told that he was also near to starvation-point, or that he was delirious and barely conscious.

Watson himself was not in a state to tell us much that might explain Hutton's condition. They had not been taken to Bridge House but to Jessfield Road, the Gendarmerie Headquarters in the Western District. He and Hutton had been confined in separate cells and he only knew what he had been able to pick up from the grapevine. It appeared, however, that Hutton had been driven to madness by the treatment that he had received and had been in that condition for some days prior to his release. There was also some suggestion that he had attacked the Japanese, but whether this was before or after being driven mad was not clear. Whatever the reason, Hutton had been stripped and then bound tightly hand and foot, never being untied for any purpose. It was left to his cell mates to feed him if they would and could. It appeared probable that he had taken neither food nor drink for some days past.

We carried him up to the isolation room and there I left him with the nursing staff who started to clean him up. When I got back downstairs, the place was in a ferment. Everyone was terribly incensed over Hutton's condition and the Colonel had added fuel to the flames by sending renewed orders that the tree raising must be resumed immediately. The loudly expressed opinion was that the Colonel knew just what he could do with his damned tree and that if he did not like it he could lump it. This was just the sort of explosive situation that gave Henningsen and myself our premature grey hairs. We knew that it was absolutely useless to attempt to try to get the men back to work in their present frame of mind, which we fully shared, but on the other hand, the Colonel had given us a direct order in person, a thing he very seldom did. He had given the order in the presence of his own troops and could not lose face by letting us get away with it. The only thing to do was to go across and explain exactly what the situation was and to suggest that the tree be left until tempers had cooled somewhat. In any case, neither the Colonel nor Honda had seen Hutton yet, and it was most desirable that they should do so in order that they might realize that our indignation was well founded.

The Colonel was in a temper and would not see us, so we had to deal first with Honda. We told him what the situation was, and that he had better see Hutton and then report to the Colonel. We neither could nor would do anything until this had been done and then we wanted to see the Colonel himself.

I went back to see how Hutton was getting on. By now he had been cleaned up and a more careful examination had been made. It looked as though before sanity had left him he had given up hope of getting out alive, and had determined to try to leave a message for us in the only way left to him — on his own body. Somehow he had managed to get hold of what was probably the broken end of a piece of wood, perhaps a piece of one of the clubs that he had been beaten with. With this he had laboriously tried to scratch words on the inside of his thighs and wrists, where it was less likely to be noticed by his captors. These words seemed to be 'Murdered', 'Killed' and several others that we could not clearly decipher. It had been his filthy state that had prevented these scratches, some of which were half an inch wide, from being seen. It is certain that he would never have been returned to us had the Gendarmerie seen them before setting him free.

In the afternoon, Henningsen and I saw the Colonel. We told him without in any way mincing our words exactly what we thought of the whole business. The camp regarded him as a soldier and a gentleman on whom they could rely for fair and honourable treatment and we were completely unable to understand how it was that he could permit a prisoner under his care to be treated in this inhuman manner. It must not be thought that we were able to talk to him in this manner with any degree of ease or freedom. We had no idea how he would react. Would he fly into a rage and order heads to roll or would he take it quietly? He had already said something about mutiny, and we were frankly scared stiff.

Fortunately he took it well, far better than I had dared to hope. We said that there was no intention in the minds of the men to refuse to carry out his orders, but that their very justifiable indignation had got the better of them. We felt that if they could be assured that the Colonel appreciated how they felt, and that he would do what lay within his power to prevent anything of this nature happening again, then we would persuade the men to resume work. I think that he was more than a little shaken himself, and he gave the required assurance almost without demur. He knew the system and had lived with it all his life, but I think it can be said that very few Japanese outside the Gendarmerie liked it.

On the day after his return, our doctors decided that the most serious feature of Hutton's condition was his mental state, which neither was qualified to treat. We therefore set about trying to arrange for him to be sent out to get treatment from a recognized alienist. Honda demurred at first, probably because he dared not let Hutton out of the camp without first obtaining the permission of the Gendarmerie, who would undoubtedly want to provide a special guard and to issue the customary warnings to the doctors and nurses in the outside hospital. Our doctors were even more anxious to get him out on account of the inteference of the Japanese medical orderlies, whom they had caught giving Hutton some injections without their knowledge. Dr Dunn had to go to Honda and threaten to have nothing whatever to do with the case and to hold the Japanese medical staff entirely responsible for whatever happened if he did not issue immediate orders that they were to leave Hutton entirely alone. Honda blustered that these orderlies were fully trained and knew just as much about medicine as any doctor, but finally had to give way.

It was not until the next day that we were able to get Hutton sent away in an ambulance to Dr Tarle's Nursing Home. He had shown no signs of improvement and on making a last examination as he was being transferred to the waiting ambulance, Dr Dunn expressed to me the doubt that he would survive the journey. He made it, but passed away on the following day. Meantime the men in the camp had agreed to get back to the job of raising the tree. The tree lived but Hutton died.

Hutton did not die in vain. Several more men were taken out for questioning after that, among them being the Judah brothers and Tiny Pitts. When told to notify them that they had to go, I reminded Honda that we did not want any repetititon of the Hutton case, and that if these men had to be questioned, there was no reason why it should take more than a few days at the outside and that the camp expected to see them come back safe and sound. That is just what happened. None of the men who were taken out after that were absent for more than a few days, nor were any of them seriously maltreated in the process.

There was an exception later on in the death of G.W. Cook, and though we were not able to prove it, we were virtually certain that his death resulted directly from ill treatment that he had received earlier on. When he returned from Gendarmerie Headquarters after some weeks of questioning he was a much changed man. Before leaving he had been hale and hearty and looked less than his years. He came back pale and thin, and looking nearer seventy than sixty. He told me that he had been questioned on his knowledge of Russian affairs. One of the conditions of his release and return to camp had been that he should write them a report on certain aspects of Soviet policy. He wanted to assure me that he would tell them nothing that was not common knowledge and he was very anxious that I should see what he ultimately wrote before he turned it over to them in order that I could exonerate him from any criticism that might fall on him after the war.

I was not too happy about this. I did not know enough about Soviet affairs to know whether or not he was revealing deep and deadly secrets, but he was in such a state that I had little option but to accede to his request. When he produced his report for my inspection, I had the feeling that if the Japanese got no more out of it than I did, they would certainly not be much the wiser.

Cook's health declined fast, and some months later we had to ask permission to send him to the Ward Road Hospital. Here he died after a few weeks from a supposed liver ailment. Sturton was very anxious to be allowed to go there to perform an autopsy as he was far from satisfied as to the accuracy of the reported cause of death. The permission was not granted and the true reason for Cook's death was buried with him.

16

FAREWELL TO THE AMERICANS

DESPITE many heart-rending scenes of the kind I have described, there occasionally shone a ray of light to relieve our spirits: the repatriation of our United States and Canadian friends was one.

The thought of repatriation had been our chief solace through all our troubles. We realized that it would be a tremendous job, but we never doubted that it would come one day, and that when it did, the Haiphong Road Camp would top the list. Rumours were many, particularly as we had so few means of verifying them. W.G. Braidwood, who had taken on the Chairmanship of the B.R.A. when I was interned, was able to get into the camp occasionally and although repatriation was a forbidden topic, I usually managed to exchange a few words with him *sotto voce* and the first illicit question was always a request for the latest news of repatriation.

It was not until late August 1943 that Honda sent for Henningsen and myself and told us that the terms under which repatriation would take place had been agreed in principle and that the first exchange would probably be for American and Canadians at a date not yet fixed. He had classification lists, giving the order of priority of the various categories which he wished us to study. I had to type interminable copies of this secretly in his office. Until matters were further advanced, we were not to mention it to other internees. This was in line with our own views. It would have been cruel to make any announcement until it was definitely settled, in case some hitch should occur.

At last, word came through that a date in mid-September had been fixed for the exchange of United States and Canadian internees. Although nothing was certain, it was expected that there would be sufficient accommodation on the exchange vessel for all the Americans and Canadians in our camp who wished to go. The only difficulty we anticipated was in the case of those men with non-American wives or dependents, since the latter would not be granted admission to the US. These men were left with a very difficult choice to make. Should they go alone to the US where they could at least be of some value to the war effort, or did their duty lie with their wives and families, for whom they could do nothing at the moment, but who might stand very much in need of their help when the war ended? About twenty of them, mostly ex-servicemen, elected to stay.

It was not until three days before the sailing date that the nominal lists for repatriation came into the camp. Five American names were immediately conspicuous by their absence: Paul Hopkins, President of the Shanghai Power Co.; Bishop Ralph Ward of the American Methodist Church; Bruce Jenkins, a local insurance man; Hillaire du Berrier, a free-lance journalist; and Giovannini whose principal claim to fame appeared to be some eminence in American Masonic circles. Henningsen thought at first that it was just a mistake, and the camp authorities were none the wiser. He was allowed to telephone the Swiss Consulate who had already made enquiries. It appeared that the Japanese had raised some undisclosed objections to the release of these men and that negotiations were still proceeding. They should maintain themselves in readiness to leave although their release was far from certain.

The eve of sailing arrived and still no news of them. Baggage inspection began. All heavy luggage was taken to the open ground in front of the Japanese office and there examined by a special Customs gang brought in for the purpose, assisted by members of the Gendarmerie. Everything was turned out and inspected in the minutest detail. One man had been foolish enought to think he could get away with a double bottom to his trunk. It was very fortunate that he had concealed there nothing more incriminating than photos of his wife and children. Even so, they gave him quite a rough passage.

There was still no news for the doubtful ones by the following morning. Their feelings cannot well be imagined. Everyone was up early. A special breakfast was served to the repatriates at 5.30 a.m. It was a special treat, bacon and eggs, fried bread and coffee. I had that last meal with Anker and Arnhold Kiehn, and had almost as much difficulty in forcing it down as they.

Finally they formed up in the driveway and marched out of the gate to the waiting trucks and buses, whilst our band gave the 'Roll out the Barrel' and 'Aloha'. There was many a moist eye on both sides and our feelings were definitely mixed. Pleasure for their sake, sorrow at parting with good friends, and the hope that our turn would not be long delayed. They may not have been allowed to carry written messages, but many of them had memorized the names and addresses of families to whom they would write when they got back to civilization. Ralphe, a lanky Canadian, did it for me. Up to that time I had only been allowed to write one letter to my wife and I could only begin to imagine how anxious she must be getting.

I know of at least one written message that was smuggled out. This was a complete list of names and connections of all men in the camp together with a report on important details of camp organization. Henningsen had had a small folding canvas chair made for himself for use on the ship. One of the cross-pieces was hollowed out and notes hidden inside. Henningsen did not know about it until he got on to the *Gripsholm*, which was just as well for his peace of mind.

We were quite confident that our turn would come next now that the ice had been broken. We hoped against hope for month after month. Every man who went to hospital carefully noted the position and condition of the big Italian liner *Conte Verde* which was the logical vessel to use. Every touch with a paint brush was the signal for renewed hope. I don't think that we really and finally gave up until the first Italian collapse, when the *Conte Verde*, that superb Lloyd Triestino liner, was scuttled in the river by her own crew.

Life quickly returned to normal humdrum routine after the departure of the Americans and Canadians. We were able to rearrange ourselves a bit and get a little more space. Even then we had an average of only 28 square feet of floor space per man inclusive of passageways. Seven feet by four is all right for a short railway journey, but it is not too much for three years. We were at last able to move the Taikoo Dockyard crowd from a hallway into proper rooms. These twelve men had been captured on 9 December 1941, when their ship was barely a day out of Hong Kong. They had been kept in Amoy for about six months and had finally been brought to us. They were all technicians and a good bunch, and had formed a very welcome addition to our numbers.

The British were now in a great majority and when it came to election of a successor to Henningsen, L. Wright of the Eagle and Globe Steel Co. was chosen by a substantial majority. He proved to be an excellent choice and we got on extremely well together. Perhaps that was in no small measure due to the fact that he stated from the outset that although in theory we two were on full equality in respect of our duties and responsibilities, he regarded me as the senior partner. Although he took the lead in many activities, he would not strike out on any new line of action or policy without first discussing it with me.

He and Jimmy Forbes came to live in the office in place of Henningsen and Kiehn. Since Jimmy as Camp Cashier and Accountant spent most of his time in the office anyway, it was a convenient arrangement. Living in the office had its advantages and disadvantages. It was light and airy and we had plenty of space when we shut down for the day and unstacked our beds. On the other hand, it meant that we were never really off-duty. Anyone with a problem to settle knew just where to find us, including the Japanese.

Relations and routine with the Japanese guard had become fairly stabilized. We were not being paraded as prize exhibits before notables quite so often, and they were beginning to realize that we were a moderately normal species of human being!

Honda himself was our biggest trouble. The Colonel paid a daily visit to the camp, but we saw little of him. His chief vice was laziness, 'anything for a quiet life' was his motto and the easiest way out for him was to leave everything possible to Honda and his subordinates. He did not really become difficult until he was ordered by his doctor to quit drinking. He did not cut it out entirely but his temper suffered considerably.

He found that I had done a bit of game shooting locally and insisted thereafter in regarding me, quite erroneously, as an expert. He frequently sent for me to ask my advice about his guns and ammunition and to tell me about his daily bag. One day he produced a .22 rifle of German make which he had recently bought and which was not performing properly. I made some small adjustment, aided by a spot of oil and then he insisted on trying it out on the adjoining range. I made a nine inch target with a two inch bull on a sheet of paper and stuck it up at a range of seventy-five yards. It must have been a really good rifle, for I put the sighting shot an inch from the bull and the second slap in the middle! Nothing he could do would persuade me to fire it again. I could not afford to spoil that bull's-eye reputation.

Although I did not enjoy my contacts with him, I felt that it was politic to be on good terms and I am sure that it proved helpful. For one thing, it helped to keep Honda in his place.

Honda was quite a different character. He had spent a few years in the US as representative of a small export house handling cheap china, toys, etc. and had picked up a smattering of the language. That is probably why he had been chosen for the job. Unlike the other officers, NCOs, and men of the guard, he did not come from the Colonel's regiment, and this left him very much on his own. He felt very keenly the terrible weight of responsibility on his shoulders, and was scared stiff of making a mistake. This meant that to him written regulations were sacred and nothing could make him amend them in the slightest detail to conform to circumstances to which they were unsuited. At times, this hit us very badly.

One of the worst instances of this was the regulation that no man was allowed to leave camp except to attend the funeral of a member of his family, or to visit a member of his family who was critically ill and expected to die. It would happen therefore that we would hear by one means or another that someone's wife was in hospital and extremely ill. After long persuasion Honda would agree to let the man out under escort and he would be permitted ten minutes of supervised conversation with the ailing wife. She would be so cheered up at seeing her husband looking fit and well that she would promptly recover. This was not according to the book and when I repeated the request later on for another case, Honda would be obdurate. He was being deceived, everybody was always giving him false information. Sick relatives were not dying as they ought and the man could not go out. It was useless to try to make him understand that half the trouble with these sick relatives was caused by worry over the fate of their menfolk, and that it was an act of elementary humanity to permit the visits. I would argue myself sick over these and similar cases, and then have the even more unhappy task of telling the unfortunate man that his request was refused. This was particularly hard on those men whose wives suffered prolonged illnesses. The mental torture that they went through must have been terrible.

The only other times when men saw their families was at the annual visits. Although it would have been far easier to take our men to the other camps, we were such dangerous people that our families had to be brought to us, sometimes in open lorries without top, sides, or backboard. These were tremendous occasions, looked forward to and prepared for for weeks ahead. Precious stores of food would be broken into to provide sandwiches and pies for the families waiting their turn, and we usually managed to turn out a good looking spread, however straightened our resources. We did not want the families to see how we usually ate.

Three rooms were placed at our disposal in the Japanese building. The interviewing room, the families' waiting room, and a small cubbyhole where the next four men up would wait their turn. This room was important to us because from time to time we were able to pass children in to their waiting fathers so that they were able to devote the whole of their precious ten minutes to their wives.

All men had to be inside our building when visitors arrived and departed. Waving or any other demonstration of affection was strictly forbidden. As if it could be! The visitors would be relieved of handbags and other offensive weapons at the guard house, and checked in by us to ensure that all had arrived, before going upstairs to the waiting room, where refreshments had been prepared.

They would then go into the interviewing room, four couples at a time, where four so-called interpreters would sit near them to ensure that they did not discuss forbidden topics such as camp conditions. Ten minutes was all that they were allowed, ten minutes, once a year. Try to cram all that you have to say in that short period and see how you like it.

In theory, no one was allowed to enter the waiting room, but in practice, Wright, Aiers, Forbes and myself as camp officials would edge in from time to time for the ostensible purpose of handing round food and many a message would then be passed out. Our biggest task perhaps was to try to persuade these anxious wives that their husbands really were speaking the truth when they said that we were not doing too badly.

There was a lighter side to these interviews as there is to nearly everything. This was the matter of common-law wives. When the question of visits from relatives was first mooted I asked Honda if visits from common-law wives would be permitted. I knew of several genuine cases and had in fact been trying to arrange marriages in order that the wives and children might receive official recognition and so qualify for relief payments from the Swiss Consulate. After some argument Honda agreed. Now in a matter of this kind one has to take the assurance of the man concerned that Miss So-and-So is his common-law wife. One had in fact no particular reason for preventing a man who had no other relatives in Shanghai from using this excuse as a means of seeing the girl-friend. Unfortunately there were apparently some rather popular girls still at large in Shanghai and one at least came in as the common-law wife of three separate men before the guards spotted her as too regular a visitor.

Our correspondence was at all times very limited. Men with relatives in Shanghai, including those interned in other camps, were allowed to write a fifty word letter to them once a month, but letters to families outside China were permitted only twice a year, and the limit for these was twenty-five words. Other camps had much greater latitude in their letters abroad, although the percentage of deliveries was so low that I doubt if they actually had many more letters reach their destination than we had.

The best way to get a letter through, if you could manage it, was to smuggle it out of the camp and have it posted in the town to a contact in Chungking (then the capital of Free China) for re-forwarding. It was an extraordinary fact that during the whole of the war it was possible to post a letter in Shanghai for delivery in Chungking which meant crossing the line between Japanese controlled China and Free China. Such letters actually arrived, without censorship, in a high percentage of cases.

Local deliveries were terribly slow and it frequently took as long as two to four months for letters written in other camps to be delivered in ours. There was naturally a great deal of dissatisfaction over this delay. Since the maximum distance between camps was something under ten miles, one could only ascribe this to bloody-mindedness on the part of the camp censor. It is difficult to imagine what news of vital import could be exchanged between husbands and wives in different camps to justify this careful scrutiny of all mail, but this was the Japanese rule.

17

OUR GARDEN AND LIVESTOCK

IN the late winter of our arrival in camp we had started a garden. This, being something productive, was heartily approved of by the Japanese and they even helped to provide us with tools. There was no free space within the compound proper, unless we dug up the little patch in front of the building. This was too small to be usefully productive, and too valuable as an exercise ground to be put to this purpose. When the Fourth Marines had occupied the building they had two adjoining plots of land for use as parade and training grounds, one on the north of about half an acre and one on the east of about one acre, which had also served as a rifle range. Both plots had been levelled out with the liberal use of brick, rubble, and garbage, covered with a layer of ash. We could not of course simply scrape off the ash and rubble and pile it on one side. This would have taken up far too much space and would also have made our land too low-lying. We had therefore to work out a system of trenching whereby we raised at least two feet of earth to the top and buried first the ashes, then the rubble as we proceeded. It was a long, slow, back-breaking job and was still going on up to the time of our being moved to Fengtai. The earth itself was very poor and sterile after being buried for so long, and was completely devoid of bacterial organisms and earthworms. Plants grew very strangely in it at first and it was not until we were leaving that the earliest dug plots were beginning to come into good tilth.

Our most useful and successful crops were Swiss chard, kohlrabi and onions. We grew lesser quantities of the more fancy crops such as tomatoes, cucumbers, beans and lettuce, more for their value as a rare treat for the men, than to provide a substantial supplement to the camp diet.

Even running a garden is not without its trials. There was a continual war on between the gardeners and the kitchen. The former wanted to see their crops come to full maturity and the latter were perpetually looking for something which would put a little taste or variety into the midday stew. As soon as the first spring onion coyly pushed a spike above ground, the cooks marked it down. From then on it was a fight all the way as to who should say just when it should be pulled. The chief cook and head gardener used to resign alternately over this perennial dispute.

Fertilizer was, of course, a big problem. The Colonel appreciated the need for manure and we were able to arrange for an occasional load to be brought in from the Scotch Dairy nearby. We had excellent contacts with the Dairy since we had in camp its two head men, Doctors Edgar and MacWhirter. Their Chinese Manager, Koo, did a very fine job for us, managing to get into camp once a month to collect payment of our milk bill. The time finally came when Koo could no longer find labour or transport for loads of manure and as our new land was just about ready for cultivation, we badly needed a few loads. To my great surprise Honda agreed to allow me to send a small gang of men under guard to the Dairy to collect and pull back a few truck loads. There was no lack of volunteers, quite the reverse, maybe they knew something that I did not. When they arrived and had loaded the truck, Koo asked if he might refresh the tired workers, and of course the guard, with a bottle of milk apiece. The milk for the men, unlike that for the guard, had been heavily laced with gin by the ever thoughtful Koo before being capped. The effect of this unaccustomed potation was to bring the truck back at the run behind a most hilarious crew, all anxious to go back for another load. I suppose the guard got jealous, for I was ordered to change the gang, and Honda gave specific instructions that under no circumstances would Dr MacWhirter be permitted to take part in any future manure manoeuvres.

One very pleasant incident resulting from our efforts at gardening was a visit from the gardening gang at the Prisoners of War Camp. They had been running into a lot of grief and the Colonel had the bright idea of bringing about a dozen of them across to us for a couple of hours under the command of Major James Devereaux of Wake Island fame.*

---

* Wake Island, a small atoll in the central Pacific, was an important US aircraft staging post, and by December 1941 was the site of a half-completed US air and submarine base. On 11 December 1941, a garrison of 520 marines with limited aircraft and defence guns, under the command of Major James Devereaux, repulsed a Japanese invasion force of six destroyers, three light cruisers and other vessels, sinking two of the destroyers. Subjected to almost continuous air attack, they held out until 23 December when the Japanese returned with a much more powerful force and forced the surrender of the island. Most of the Americans captured were then evacuated to prisoner-of-war camps in China and Japan.

They were heavily escorted and supervised, but by getting permission to give them an alfresco meal in the garden, we managed to exchange quite a lot of information. I like to think that they were as much cheered by the visit as we were.

Livestock was another subject of amusement. They may not have provided a great deal of nourishment but they certainly had a very real recreational value. It started off at Christmas 1942, our first one in the camp. A parcels truck had come in, and shortly after it had been unloaded, Hector Moffat entered the office carrying a basket of live chickens.

'These don't seem to be addressed to anyone,' he said, 'so can I have them?' He was never one to lose out for lack of asking.

I immediately recognized them as mine. There were three white Leghorns, including a cock, and three Chinese-bred hens. Moffat was only too willing to look after them, and he did it most successfully. He rigged up a chicken house and run out of a few pieces of nothing scrounged from here and there. When spring came I had two sittings of Rhode Island Reds and Plymouth Rocks sent in, just to add to the variety. Prices had already begun to soar and I had to pay about forty dollars an egg. From then on breeding seasons never found us without five or six sittings, and the young chicks provided a never-ending source of pleasure to the camp. A young chick is a pretty thing at any time and when you are as starved for pleasures as we were, the sight of a brood of chicks being introduced to life and the world by mother hen is something not to be missed. The number we could keep was governed by considerations of space and food supply. We were greatly lacking in both. This meant, among other things, that we had to kill off our surplus cockerels early and thus diminish the number of impromptu cockfights which also enlivened the camp. Moffat and I as breeders were not in favour of cockfights as we could not afford to let our male stock damage itself.

The apportionment of eggs was a bit of a problem and was finally solved by giving up to ten a day to the hospital patients, and distributing the remainder to the camp. This on average gave each man in the camp a new laid egg once every two or three months. Not often, but very welcome when it came.

We really came to know each hen by name and habit. So much so that when we came to leave and had to kill them off, I had to get Jimmy Jackson to do the job. Buck Taylor had by then become chief chicken nurse and neither he nor Moffat could bring himself to kill them.

Bees we had too, but they never gave us a scrap of honey, in spite of consuming substantial quantities of our precious sugar during the winter months. The hives were beautifully made in camp by Capt. Jeaune, and we derived a lot of pleasure from the lectures on beekeeping given by A.E. Thornton and from following them up on the bees in person. I am afraid we were asking too much expecting them to produce honey in the middle of wartime Shanghai.

Our rabbits definitely did not do well. They ate largely and reproduced to order, but what with weasels and a high rate of mortality they were never a worthwhile contribution to the camp larder. We found too that when a doe was bearing progeny which, rabbit fashion was just about always, we were required to approach the warren on tiptoe, if at all, and to speak in whispers so that really they had not much value as a spectacle.

The pigs fared rather better, although we were never really fond of them as they were not wholly ours and we never knew until they were dead and ready to be eaten just how small our share actually was. This was one of Honda's ideas. For months he had talked about pigs, and his intention to bring some into camp for us. I had always tried to put him off the idea as I did not see how we could feed them properly. We no longer had overflowing swill buckets and the waste was steadily being cut down. I could moreover see the possibility of there being strong competition between the pigs and my chickens for what scraps of food there were to be had. However, Honda finally said that he had arranged to get some pigs out of a litter that was due at the Prisoners of War Camp and we were to prepare a sty for them. Many weeks later he called me to his office and said that today was the great day, the pigs would definitely arrive. It was a red-hot summer day, and when the truck arrived at about four in the afternoon, there were four miserable panting piglets lying on the bare floor in the blazing sun. Apparently they had been picked up early in the morning and had then been driven around the town on various errands for the whole day, without ever having a scrap of shade. Three of them died within an hour of their arrival in spite of everything that we tried to do to revive them. The fourth, the only male, lived and finally throve but it was touch and go for a long while.

This was a terrific loss of face for Honda. He should have four pigs on the books and could only produce one. He wasn't much concerned with the inhumanity of the treatment which had caused their death but he was very seriously worried at the hiatus in his porcine roll call. He was finally able to square it by getting a sow in farrow. She came on to the books as one pig and evened things up very nicely by producing three.

18

RECREATION

DURING our years in camp, softball was our chief form of outdoor recreation. We tried football but found it much too dangerous. Ashes make a nasty rash and healing is liable to be very slow when the standard of nutrition is below par. We soon had half a dozen softball teams, and I think we learnt quickly. We found that a good cricketer has little to learn about fielding and throwing, which is such a vital feature of the game. It took us some time to catch on to the barracking end of it. Your cricket crowd is very decorous, and a gentlemanly 'Well played, Sir' is the limit of permissible enthusiasm. Not so with the diamond game, and the Americans set out to teach us with a vengeance. One man in particular, Russel Brines, had a very irritating yodel which he produced, either when he did something clever, which was frequent, or when we did something foolish, which was even more frequent. This went on for quite a time until one day Brines himself muffed an easy one, and someone in the bleachers let out an imitation of his own patent yodel. From then on poor Brines could not do a thing without being yodelled at until he was put right off his game. I never did quite understand why Henningsen took me aside afterwards and tried to explain that that was not how it should be done.

We also managed some musical entertainment. Our concerts were really masterly affairs. There was too much work involved in their preparation for us to have them very frequently but they fully justified the effort put into them. E.G. Smith-Wright was the moving spirit, but all his efforts would have gone for naught had it not been for the wonderful work of his technical assistants and stage hands.

Our main platform was about ten feet by eight and was made from rough but solid timber filched from an old bin. The scenery was made out of newspaper, several thicknesses of which were stuck together with rice-water paste. Colouring materials were always a problem but we had red, yellow, and grey brick which when ground up made fair colour washes. Then the colours would be soaked out of socks or ties and a dash of ink thrown in. The finished effect was amazingly good. We had a couple of artists in the camp, Telfer and Van Amerongen, who designed and painted back drops. The latter was able to bring in some oil colours which he used lavishly in painting a tropical scene on the usual glued newspapers. This was used over and over again with slight modifications.

The real ingenuity came in the stage properties and in the lighting and sound effects. These were really beautifully done. We have had a fountain playing on the stage, moving chariots, and on one occasion in a cabaret scene, at a wave from the head waiter, the orchestra travelled slowly backwards on a mobile platform to make way for the dancers.

This sort of thing may not sound much to a hardened theatregoer, but we, knowing the limitations under which our stage hands worked, were as thrilled as a bunch of schoolboys seeing their first play.

The majority of our shows were of the musical revue type since these presented less difficulties. We only put on two straight plays, 'Outward Bound', an obvious choice because of its all male cast, and Oscar Wilde's 'The Importance of Being Earnest'.

By the time we came to put on what proved to be our last show, we ran into considerable difficulties with the lighting. Very strict orders had been issued about the conservation of electric power, which was not to be used for any mechanical device, or for any unnecessary purpose. A stage show was regarded by Honda as an unnecessary purpose, and although we offered to make it up by going without lights in the building completely for one night, he would not relent. We thought at first that this would put us off completely. Candles were the only possibility and they were extremely expensive, hard to get, and we had practically no money. However, our technicians, after making tests, decided that they could get by with only a dozen candles cut into short lengths and set in tin reflectors. The show duly took place, with Honda and the Quartermaster sitting in the middle of the front row. The lighting was really superb, far better than I could have thought possible from a few candle ends and home-made tin reflectors. After the show I congratulated Geoff Forrestier and the stage hands on their marvellous lighting effects. I thought that there was a suggestion of a snigger in their acceptance of my compliments but it was not until later that they told me they had been using concealed electric lighting to supplement the candles right under Honda's nose.

The Japanese, not to be outdone, had their own ways of keeping us amused. The chief of these was the periodic search. Electrical devices as a whole were forbidden, and they were always in deadly fear that we might have a concealed radio or two about the place. They would descend on us unannounced, order everyone to their rooms, post sentries in every corridor and passageway and set to work. The intensity and thoroughness of the searches varied but generally they went through every single thing we had. Lt. Miyazaki, more commonly known as 'Dog Face', was the worst of the bunch. One never knew what he would decide was a contraband possession. There was one notable occasion when he realized that there was a lot more wooden furniture around the place than could properly be accounted for. We started off with nothing but our beds and baggage, no chairs, tables or benches or anything of that kind. Naturally every man who could beg, borrow or steal a hammer and a few nails lost no time in scrounging a few pieces of timber from some part of the structure and constructed himself a set of furniture. Dog Face took a sudden dislike to this and started passing every bit of such furniture out to the waiting sentries, who carted it off. The men were pretty angry at this, and then somebody started to laugh. This drove Dog Face into a complete frenzy. He frothed at the mouth and threw discretion completely to the wind. From then on everything went straight out of the windows to fall crashing into the courtyard below. The sentries became completely disorganized and stuff began to be passed back from rooms yet unsearched to those that had already been visited and men even began to filch things back from the heap of debris in the yard. Dog Face carried on grimly until even he became exhausted and had to give up.

The banning of the use of electrical appliances did not of course put an automatic end to their use. It simply meant increased skill in their concealment. Room 26, an American room, had probably the best device. It was certainly the one which lasted longest. They cut a small trapdoor in their floor, hinged it, and fastened their hotplate to the underside. They arranged their electrical connection in such a way that it cut automatically as soon as the trap door was shut. At the first sign of danger, all they had to do was to kick the trapdoor over and be left with no evidence but the frying pan in their hand which, of course, came straight from the kitchen. They even took their current by tapping the main power line outside, so that their extensive use of electricity should not show up on the meter.

Another form of amusement greatly favoured by 'Dog Face' was the bowing parade. The order was that we should bow to any Japanese officer or NCO or any sentry on duty whenever we passed them. This, of course, was a tedious and unpopular form of exercise and was seldom indulged in. We were in particular expected to bow to the Colonel when he arrived on his daily visit. His car would hoot when he was well down the road, which gave the guard time to turn out, whilst our part was to remain stationary wherever we happened to be, and bow towards our own little ray of rising sun as he entered the archway. This was simply not being done, so 'Dog Face' decided to take us in hand.

Each day at roll-call he would make each room bow a dozen or more times before passing on to the next room. With breakfast waiting this was very unpopular and we did not enjoy being pulled about by him to make us adopt the correct attitude of respect. If he was not satisfied with the performance at roll-call he would order special bowing parades. He further altered the orders in respect of our behaviour when the Colonel arrived. In future, instead of simply remaining where we happened to be, we must run forward and line the avenue from the gateway to the office, and bow delicately from the hips as his honour passed. The only result of this was that whenever the toot of the horn was heard, there would be a mad rush to get into the building and under cover before the car reached the gateway. The Colonel must frequently have wondered whether we had not all gone home during the night.

I personally could not avoid doing a great deal of bowing. I had to make obeisance before and after I approached a Japanese on a matter of business, which was many times a day. When the rest of the chaps were sitting round and saying what they couldn't do with a nice thick steak when they met one, I was longing for the day when I could hire a small boy to walk behind me and give me a swift kick in the rear every time my back departed from the vertical.

I must not give the impression that planned work and recreation alone were sufficient to keep us fit. That would be casting an unmerited slight on our camp medical service. Sturton, with the help of 'Doc' Craddock and Ronnie Hillman, had to train a full complement of men to nurse all those patients whom we retained in camp in preference to sending them outside. Since, towards the end, the sole night staff at the Gaol Hospital consisted of two Chinese boys who were compelled to pull rickshaws during the day in order to survive, no one went outside who could avoid doing so. Sturton himself was far from well and we were at times gravely concerned over him, although he was never off his feet for long. His band of helpers became devoted to him. H.R.O. Edmonds was one of them. He had a chemical background, and did wonders using an old microscope and improvising on stains used for examining specimens.

Camp health in general remained really very good. Although there were a number of tragic deaths, our mortality rate was somewhat lower than the average for normal life outside. I think that the deaths of W. J. Monk and P. A. Austen were the only ones which actually occurred within the confines of the camp. We felt it desirable, in the interests of camp morale, to transfer the very sick to the Gaol Hospital when it was apparent that there was nothing more we could do for their comfort. It sounds a little callous, perhaps it was.

For some reason Austen's funeral took place direct from the camp. None of us were allowed to go out, but we lined the central avenue as the hearse went down towards the gate. Hanvey played 'Taps'. He had been in the Marine Band and could make a trumpet do everything but talk. For Austen he excelled himself. Some simple scenes are unforgettable, perhaps because of their very simplicity.

We had no serious epidemics, a few sporadic outbreaks of dysentery, and one fairly bad go of flu which did not however sweep through the camp as might have been anticipated from our crowded conditions. We were fortunately spared malaria. Our camp situation had not much to recommend it, hemmed in as it was by Chinese houses, but at least it was not a malarial district and I do not think we had a single case of original infection. This is not to say that we were free from mosquitoes. There were enormous ones which must have measured nearly one inch from nose to tail.

Mosquitoes were by no means our worst insect pest. The place of honour undoubtedly went to the bed bugs. The building was known to be infested with them when we arrived and we must have proved a very welcome source of nourishment to these hungry hordes. There seemed to be no effective means of getting rid of them, short of physical removal of all those that could be seen, but there were always enough left behind to propagate a new flock in a very few days. One might have thought that putting the legs of beds in tins of disenfectant would hold them back, but they were not defeated by any little obstacle like that. They simply crawled up the wall and across the ceiling and dropped down from above!

The one saving grace about these little pests was that they were very selective in their eating. I was one of the unfortunates, they were awfully fond of me. No mosquito net was fine enough to keep them from my delectable carcass.

19

EVENTS ESCALATE

FOR the first few months we were allowed a radio with local reception only. The best news came from the local Russian station. By arrangement with the Japanese, they were allowed to comment fully on the situation in the West, provided that they confined themselves to the Japanese version of events in the East. A similar situation obtained when the use of the radio was stopped and we were limited to the Japanese edited version of the *Shanghai Times*. They would print quite freely dispatches from Berlin, London and Washington dealing with the European picture, which must have been very galling to the local German community. We were thus kept quite reasonably up-to-date on half of the global war picture.

Probably the one factor which more than any other contributed to the maintenance of camp morale at a high level was this outside picture. We were interned on the eve of the Battle of El Alamein, by which time we had suffered and absorbed the shocks of our worst disasters. If the news in the Far East continued to be gloomy, it was at least counterbalanced by successes in the West.

Events in the Pacific were more difficult to piece together, and we had to do a great deal of reading between the lines. As long as the Japanese were advancing, their reports were reasonably factual. There was no need for deceit. But when they were stopped, or pushed back, they had to bring their imagination into play. Fortunately their imaginations were so thoroughly stereotyped as to defeat their purpose. The attack on Imphal in Burma was a typical instance. They advanced towards it, threw out their enveloping flanks, and then started to 'tighten the iron ring around Imphal'. For days and weeks they went on tightening that much worn and strained iron ring, long after it had become completely obvious that either the metal was defective, or it was not a ring. They did not drop this well worn phrase until they were able to report a glorious victory and rapid pursuit of the retreating enemy a considerable distance to the south. From then on their victorious battles bcame even more numerous and more heroic, but always a bit nearer home. We really began to look forward to their victories. The situation in the Pacific was much the same, they claimed to have inflicted enormous losses on the United States fleet in every encounter until it had been sunk three times over long before the battle of Leyte.

Our other principal source of news on local and more personal matters was the International Red Cross. We were fortunate in having Molly Foyne as the official representative assigned to work for our camp. Twice a month the I.R.C. were allowed to send Molly into camp with a truck bringing parcels and supplies. We were permitted to correspond with the I.R.C. on a limited range of subjects and to ask them to carry out certain services for us. Molly would therefore bring a batch of correspondence with her, which had of course to be censored before we could receive it, and would collect the outgoing mail for the I.R.C. We were allowed to discuss certain matters with her, which had first to be submitted to the Japanese for approval. Henningsen and I, and later Wright and I, would always make a point of going into the Japanese office together to meet Molly. A chance would almost invariably arise for one of us to divert the attention of the Japanese by starting an argument, whilst the other would chat idly with Molly. These idle chats gave us information which, although not normally of vital importance to the camp as a whole, was of great importance to some individual. She would for instance make a point of visiting the General Hospital when she knew there were relatives there, and would bring us first-hand reports on their condition. Honda would not allow such reports to come in by official I.R.C. mail, as he thought it might upset the men too much. This was typical of his purely negative outlook on many of our problems.

The only trouble with Molly was that she went too far and too fast in her endeavours to help us. She took risks that left us in a cold sweat. In the end, she suddenly stopped coming in with the truck, and we heard that she was sick and had had to resign her job. I cannot imagine her ever doing that, and believe she must have been warned off. I hope it was nothing worse than that because we all owe her a debt that we can never repay.

We received two consignments of Red Cross parcels whilst we were in camp. The first in 1943, before the repatriation of the Americans, and the second in the winter of 1944. The food parcels were magnificent, particularly those packed in America. Whoever made them up showed rare sympathy and understanding of what would most appeal to people long deprived of the ordinary amenities of life. We gathered that they were intended to be fortnightly issues. We felt that one of them every two months would have enabled us to live like fighting cocks.

The Japanese looked on these parcels with a very jealous eye indeed. They were a real eye-opener to them. When the first lot came in, we were told by Lt. Honda that the job of guarding them and the labour of handling and transport had proved a very onerous and tiring task for the members of our small garrison and that it would prove not merely gracious, but probably a very wise gesture on our part to present a package to each soldier, and two to the Colonel. After all, more consignments would be coming in due course, and we should not want anything untoward to happen to them. Colonel Ashworth, the senior officer of the POW camp, had already taken this enlightened view, and we should certainly not want to be less generous than he. Strangely enough too, just enough parcels had arrived to enable us to make this wise and generous gesture without depriving any inmate of his due quantity. Put like that, how could we find the heart to refuse?

The camp finances often provided us with some pretty problems, but the less money we had to deal with, the simpler our problems became. In the winter of 1944, when Comfort Allowances stopped altogether, we were advised that one more large remittance would come through for medical expenses. Hitherto, we had submitted bills for approved medical expenses to the Swiss Consulate, and they had paid the professional men concerned direct. These had been for special treatment for a few cases on which Sturton felt that he needed help, but mainly for occulists and dental work. A Japanese dentist visited the camp about once a week and did useful work. He would quote us for a denture job, we would approve the figure and authorize him to go ahead. By the time he came to finish the job, perhaps several months later, prices would have advanced so much that he would find himself out of pocket. If we did not agree to increase his fee he just would not finish the job, which was very unfortunate for the man whose teeth had been taken out. Not that teeth were needed very much on our diet.

When our remittance arrived, it proved greatly in excess of our immediate needs. However, it was quite certain that at the existing rate of depreciation, the money would lose at least half its purchasing power in under four months. We could not bear to see the money go to waste. The answer was, quite literally, peanuts. We decided to invest in a commodity that would store well, and that would be readily saleable both inside and outside the camp. We could sell peanuts in bulk whenever cash was needed, or we could pay the dentist in peanuts, or for use in the camp we could make peanut butter very satisfactorily in the big mincer lent to us by our friends in the Scotch Dairy. It worked like a charm. Finance certainly has all sorts of angles and we met and dealt with a great many of them.

One of the less pleasant episodes of this period concerned the men's petition to the Swiss Consulate asking to be allowed to rejoin wives and families interned in other camps. The fact that we had for some unexplained reason been treated differently from all other internees and had been separated from our families was a constant source of discontent and complaint. Representations on this subject to the Swiss Consulate or the I.R.C. were absolutely forbidden. The matter was raised many times with Honda, and a petition had been addressed to the Colonel. There was no reply beyond the statement that the matter could not be discussed, and we had no reason to believe that he had passed on our grievance to higher quarters.

Feeling finally grew to such a pitch that the men felt strongly that a final effort must be made in the form of a letter addressed to the Swiss Consulate with a covering note to the Colonel asking him to forward it on our behalf. They felt that this would put the Japanese on the spot, compel them either to do as we asked, or officially to refuse to forward a communication to our Protecting Power.

The letters were duly drawn up and signed, and I presented them to Honda, in not too happy a frame of mind. I was pretty sure that some sort of an explosion would follow. He reminded me that the presentation of petitions of this nature was absolutely forbidden, and refused to receive it. Wright and I equally refused to take it back. If the Japanese did not want to act on it, that was their affair, but we insisted that they at least accept it or give us a written refusal to act on it. Neither side would give way, and Wright and I did not want to leave and just find the letter dropped back on our desk later on. I suggested, therefore, that Honda should see the men himself and state his position. They would at least then know that we had done our best. There were always some in the camp who, when we had to report the failure of a mission of this kind, were far from satisfied that we had pressed the case as energetically as we might, and we did not wish there to be any doubt this time.

The meeting started fairly quietly in the front hall, with Honda standing behind the table customarily used for Captains' meetings. Then Bishop Curtis took a hand in the proceedings and acted as spokesman for the group. Curtis, a man of sixty-odd, was full of obstinate Irish courage which made him a very doughty champion, but a terribly poor negotiator. Before long, Honda was just longing to fly at Curtis' throat, and was only deterred by the latter's age and cloth. He had to have a victim, however, and when Collinson in reply to some statement by Honda said: 'But isn't that rather inhumane?', he leapt down from the table on which he was by now standing in order to shout at us better, charged into the crowd, and slapped Collinson hard in the face. Collinson had the good sense and courage to stand perfectly still and not to attempt to retaliate. Anything might have happened if he had. That broke up the meeting very effectively. Honda rushed out with a face like thunder and we settled back to await developments.

We were kept in suspense for a few hours before Bishop Curtis, Wright and myself were sent for. We were escorted upstairs to the Colonel's office and found him sitting bolt upright behind his desk with a dirty look in his eye. No sitting in easy chairs this time, we were lined up in front of him. He bowed. We stood to attention, very naughty boys indeed. He then proceeded to read from a large volume in front of him, whilst Honda translated. These were apparently the Japanese version of the regulations for the treatment of Prisoners of War.

'For disobedience to an officer, 10 to 25 years imprisonment.'

'For striking an officer, 10 years imprisonment or death.'

'For incitement to mutiny, 25 years imprisonment or death.'

For ten minutes he picked out all the most heinous crimes and grisly punishments. Then he concentrated on Bishop Curtis, and told him what he thought of him and what he had the power to do to him. The Bishop, as obstinate and full of fight as ever, answered back whilst the Colonel became more and more enraged. I was in an absolute agony of apprehension, not for myself, for I knew that it was Curtis who was now being made the scapegoat. I realized too that the Colonel's intention had originally been to do no more than scare the Bishop, but that if he were goaded a fraction more, he would lose all control and would do just what he threatened. I could finally contain myself no longer and shouted at Curtis: 'For God's sake shut up!'

It seemed at last to penetrate and he subsided, muttering to himself. The Colonel cooled off too, and shortly thereafter we were dismissed. That was the last we heard of it, for which I was very profoundly thankful. Such episodes were altogether too hard on the nerves.

Our last winter in Shanghai was bitterly cold. Our ration of two tons of coal a month made cooking and tea making alone a matter of the utmost difficulty and left nothing whatever for heating. We had a small store of carefully concealed hard coal left, with which we were able to provide a quick hot shower once a week. Water pressure had fallen very low and we had to fill our roof tank, thirty-odd feet up, by pumping it up by hand with a very fine long barrelled double-action pump constructed by our Taikoo engineers.

We were not the only people short of fuel. The whole town was short. Factories were shut down, power and gas output was greatly restricted, and domestic consumption was at a very low level. No longer were the Shanghai skies blanketed by a pall of smoke and the cold struck straight down on to us. I used to keep a thermometer just inside the opened window of the office, which was also our bedroom. It was below freezing point in the morning for sixty-five consecutive days. Several times it was around the 16 degrees Fahrenheit mark which was very low for Shanghai, and particularly low to an undernourished body living in unheated premises. Every move outside had to be made at the double in an effort to keep warm. Office work became extremely difficult, and I was really sorry for the men who were doing our typing, and trying to write up the account books. No quantity of newspapers and overcoats seemed to keep one warm at night. Frequent trips to the lav were the order of the day, or rather night and that was a long, cold walk. Some men got over this difficulty by taking a small can to bed with them. I still think that Bulpin played a very dirty trick on a room-mate by puncturing the bottom of his can with a nail.

I think the worst feature of that winter for me was the chilblains. Perhaps they were due to some dietary deficiency in addition to the cold, but certainly many men who had never had them before or since suffered severely. The lucky ones only had them on their hands, the real unfortunates were those who got them on their feet, so badly that they could not walk at all.

We had begun to have an occasional air raid which cheered us up immensely. The only thing about the air raids that I really did not like was the air-raid practices. The Japanese took these very seriously and expected us to co-operate. When there was a genuine raid on, they were far too busy looking after themselves to bother about us, other than to ensure that we were all safely locked in. The trouble with the practices occurred when Honda decided that a bomb had set fire to the roof of the kitchen and that we must go through the motions of putting it out. We had to conscript a fire brigade of about ten men to join in the festivities as part of the routine. They sometimes had fun as they were permitted to operate a couple of stirrup pumps, and much laughter and games can result from a misdirected jet of water. The real trouble came when Honda decided that the water main had been cut and all hands must turn out to form a chain of buckets. This the men simply would not do in spite of my pleading to them to get it over and done with. Then Honda would get mad and send in two or three of the troops to round them up, or, if he got mad enough to acquire a bit of courage, he might even come himself and try to chase them out. I expect it was really funny but I was always afraid of the spark that might set off the explosion that always underlay such contacts between the men and the Japanese.

Their own equipment was ludicrous. They had no hoses, about ten buckets, most of which leaked, four or five stirrup pumps of which only three worked, but they had some nice wet straw mats and a couple of mops on long bamboo poles of which they thought very highly.

As a matter of fact we took the danger very seriously and our own private practices were quite different affairs. We had four very well trained first aid stretcher squads, most of whom passed their St. John's Ambulance Corps test in the camp, and we contrived a great deal of equipment and first aid gear. We were preparing for the possibility not only of air-raid damage, but also of an eventual attack on the town by liberating troops. We set up a water filtration and sterilization plant, salvage gangs, and all the organization for rapid evacuation of the building, not only of personnel, but also of as many valuable stores and personal effects as possible. Each man had his escape kit containing emergency rations and a change of clothing, and constantly kept his personal effects stowed in a way that would permit rapid removal of the most important possessions. Although these preparations were never utilized for the purpose for which they were intended, they were in fact of considerable value when we came to be transferred to Fengtai. Their real value was in the very marked morale uplift that they provided.

20

DEPARTURE, DESTINATION UNKNOWN

EARLY in May 1945 the news came that the Prisoners of War Camp at Kiangwan was being transferred to Japan. Colonel Odera went with them, and we were left with Honda in sole charge. This was very ominous. Honda still denied that there was any possibility of our being shifted also, but there was scant doubt in our minds that such would be our fate. There was, of course, just the faint possibility that the camp would be broken up and men allowed to rejoin their wives, but we felt in our hearts that this was mere wishful thinking.

A few weeks later, twelve men were brought into camp to swell our numbers. They were all former members of the POW Camp at Kiangwan who had been left behind on account of sickness or disability. All but one were Americans, and several were Marines.

Some were still far from fit and remained hospital cases as long as they were with us. A few days after they arrived, they were paraded before Honda who told them that since it had been found necessary to attach them to a civilian internment camp, and it was against all the rules to have military and civilian prisoners in one camp, the Japanese Government had decided to demobilize them! Henceforth therefore, they were no longer members of any military force but were simply civilians. It was as simple as that. They should have sent Honda to the battlefields, I mused, preferably to Leyte where the Japanese were in the process of losing the war. He would only have had to stand up in No Man's Land and tell the opposing American forces that the Japanese Government had decided to regard them all as civilians, and they would all have said 'Hooray' and gone home.

During the first week in June our orders came. About the middle of the month we were to be transferred by rail to an unspecified destination. We would be permitted to take all personal baggage and camp equipment, provided that the total did not prove excessive and that transport could be provided.

122

The first thing that we asked for was that men should be permitted to see their families before leaving. This was refused on the grounds that there was no time. The second was that in view of the relatively large numbers of sick and aged men in the camp, coaches should be allotted to us instead of goods wagons. Honda arranged this, but I am not sure it was a good move, since it was made the excuse for cutting down the number of vehicles allotted to us and for crowding us unmercifully.

We received permission to send out of the camp for storage any personal effects that we did not wish to take with us and to send surplus equipment to the I.R.C. for distribution to other camps. Then the packing started. Three hundred men dependent on their own resources need a mountain of gear. We did not even know where we were going, or what we would find when we got there. We could not risk leaving behind any essential item of equipment. Medical and dental equipment and stores, carpenters and plumbers tools and supplies, office and kitchen equipment, it amounted to a great volume, in contrast to the dearth of lumber for packing cases.

It was hot work too. June is not one of Shanghai's kindest months and we perspired in rivers. The final date was set. We should have two days for loading at the station, and would leave on 16 June. Five goods waggons would be allotted to us. Honda said that he had had a row with the Army railway authorities by demanding coaches for personal accommodation and that the five wagons would now have to take the garrison gear as well as ours. We still did not know what size wagon would arrive. All that we could do therefore was to grade our gear in order of importance and if necessary, leave behind whatever we could not get aboard.

It was not until two days before we left that Honda produced the list of men who would be left behind. It was then that we discovered it consisted entirely of men at the Gaol Hospital, and that no consideration whatever appeared to have been given to the twenty-odd men in our camp hospital. Honda knew perfectly well that unless they were surgical, our most serious cases were left in camp where nursing and care were of a very high order indeed. He had simply forgotten them. We really were gravely concerned over this error. We had a number of serious heart conditions on our hands, men who had to be spared the least exertion and excitement, and several other medical cases whose treatment required the greatest care. Sturton, Wright and I therefore decided that we should be failing in our duty if we did not make our protest in writing against the action of the Japanese in forcing these men to undergo an ordeal which might well prove fatal to them. I do not remember the precise phraseology of the letter. It was brief and straightforward, and at some point contained the words 'inhuman treatment'.

We had recently had a new Japanese doctor posted to the camp. Although he only held the rank of sergeant major he had been a professor in the medical section of Tokyo University. Perhaps he was soured because of his low rank, but we certainly found that he possessed a very foul temper. His ire was aroused by the wording of our letter. He sent for us. We found him sitting behind his desk, leaning his chin on the large and deadly looking knob on top of his walking stick. He started off quietly enough. We were gentlemen. We were men of some education. We understood the meaning of words and their full import. The word human was known to us, also perhaps the word inhuman.

His voice had been rising steadily as this catechism proceeded and now it became an absolute screech. It was only now that we gathered what he was driving at as he thrust our letter of protest in our faces and pointed to the offending words. Then he let loose a torrent of Japanese which quite defeated Endo's efforts to interpret. He stamped and raved and shook his stick at us until I was sure that he would end up having an attack. Finally he managed to contain himself and ended up with a roar:

'Get out. Get out', crashing his stick down on the desk in front of him. Out we got.

We were somewhat shaken, and more than a little worried. This was the sort of jam in which we were too often being placed. This man was to be our medical officer for the journey and we might have to depend on him for a great deal. We were jointly responsible for the welfare and safety of some three hundred men, and was it right to allow a matter of principle to jeopardize their wellbeing? We decided we should placate him somewhat, without however withdrawing our protest completely. We therefore submitted another letter in which we simply made a formal protest without other comment. Fortunately he fell sick soon after this and had to be dosed by Sturton, which eased the situation somewhat.

Loading began. Steve Mills was in charge of the gangs working at camp, Sam Tweedie at the railway station. George Kalafatis, a Greek sea captain, supervised the actual stowage. It was terrifically hot and men worked until they fainted. The trucks were some distance from the loading platform and it was not until the end of the day that they could be moved closer. Then of course we found we were expected to load the Japanese gear first. It was no use refusing. Then Hector Moffat got himself under a falling package, was badly concussed, and had to be brought back on a stretcher. They returned to us a very tired and dispirited crew.

The International Red Cross had been able to send in a quantity of packages a few days before we left, including a hundred pounds or so of peanut butter. We felt that this together with some rusks that the Japanese had acquired, and some promised supplies of tinned food, would probably take care of our needs on the journey.

From here on all was confusion. As long as we had been able to handle the arrangements, we had been able to keep things moving at a reasonable rate with some order. Honda had resolutely refused to give us any indication whatever of the nature or capacity of the coaches that would be allotted to us. Trucks arrived, we got on. Then they wanted to count us. We stood up, we sat down, they counted and recounted, never getting the same total twice. Finally we all had to get out to be counted properly. Then we got back aboard again, but not all on the same trucks as before. Another check and more confusion. We were not all going on this convoy, three more trucks would come from the station. The convoy started. A shout came from the office. The convoy stopped. The truck drivers from the station said that they were not going to work any more today and had gone back home. We must all crowd on to these already very full ones. Somehow, after being counted yet again and several times, we all managed to get aboard and started off.

For many of us it was the first time we had been outside the confines of the camp since we first entered it nearly three years earlier. We felt rather like children being taken for our first motor car ride, and stared about us with corresponding curiosity. We saw little change in the Shanghai streets, apart from the absurd air raid shelters of mud and straw, and the funk holes dug into the pavements whose only practical use appeared to be that of serving as public lavatories. A few waves and cheers greeted us as we passed but in general the Chinese were too indifferent or cowed to make any overt demonstration.

We arrived in the station yard, stood about there for an hour or so being gaped at by the native populace who were kept at a respectful distance, and awaited orders. Then the station loading gang came in sight and joined us. They had finished their job, but what a state they were in! Dirty and absolutely worn out, but more than angry because they had not been allowed the promised return to camp for a wash and clean up.

In the midst of their expostulations it started to rain. That broke up the party. Everything for the train, all our light baggage and equipment, our food supplies, had to be got under cover. There was no difficulty in getting the men to look after our own stuff, but there was a near riot when the Quartermaster wanted the Japanese gear moved too.

Finally Honda decided that it was time we started to get on the train. We were strung out in a long irregular bunch outside the platform barrier, each man with his little pile of impedimenta. There was an hour of pushing and shoving before everyone was in their allotted places.

It was dark when we moved off and I made one sortie to see how people were settling down.

Tired as we were, sleep did not prove easy. The seats were made of split bamboo in strips. The backs rose only to shoulder height so that one's head was unsupported. We had to sleep bolt upright for four nights in a row with no change of position during the day. In at least one coach the guards would not even let the men stand up and stretch.

Morning came and found us on the outskirts of Nanking. I made a trip along the train, ignoring the sentries who tried to stop me, and began to arrange the distribution of rusks and peanut butter. Honda had said that hot tea would be provided at stations en route. But he seemed to have exhausted himself completely by the effort of getting us safely on board, and could not be bothered any further. In fact, the precious little cold water we eventually got was due entirely to the efforts of Endo, our new interpreter, who did his best for us in spite of being consistently balked at every turn.

The supplies provided by the Japanese proved to be nothing but dry biscuit. When asked about the tinned luxuries, Honda expressed deep regret: 'Could not get, but you have Red Cross parcels'. I protested, more in sorrow than in anger. I had reached a stage where I could not even get angry with him any more.

We had been greatly greatly concerned over the possibility of having to detrain and unload at Nanking for the passage over the Yangtze, and although we were sorry to see that the train ferry was still running for the military advantage, we were glad for our sakes. We crossed during the early afternoon and then spent several hours being pushed and shunted in the sidings at Pukow. We did not set off again till dusk.

The sleeping problem was ingeniously solved, for a time at least by some of the men in the second coach. There was a baggage rack above the seats. To this they slung a rope loop coming down to shoulder height. A little padding with a jacket in the bottom of the loop, and the arms could be rested thereon with elbows spread wide and the head pillowed on the outstretched arms. The slings were not rigged until well after dark, and at a time when the sentries were not being specially attentive. In due course one of them did a turn up and down the coach to make sure of our numbers. Imagine his consternation on suddenly coming across these corpse-like figures, their heads lolling drunkenly to the jerks of the train, at the end of a loop of rope. He did not even dare to touch them but tore through the train in search of the Japanese doctor. The latter, aroused from sleep, came hurrying back buttoning up his pants as he ran. He gingerly approached the nearest corpse, that of Brigadier Walker of the Salvation Army, and gave it a tentative shake. No result. It took more than that to wake a man who was enjoying his first satisfactory sleep for forty-eight hours. A more vigorous shake woke him up, rubbing his eyes and muttering at being disturbed. The Japanese doctor, realizing how he had been fooled, burst into a torrent of profanity and slapped Walker hard across the face and then proceeded to wake others similarly. From then on sleeping slings were prohibited. I was not told about this until some time later. Brigadier Walker said that they had not wanted to worry me.

The next afternoon we arrived in Tsinan where to our great pleasure we found a set of wash places and running water on the platform. Even this we were not allowed to finish, and Honda ordered us back on to the train a good hour before it moved again. Whilst we were waiting a train pulled in at the opposite platform and several of the men recognized and were able to exchange a few shouted words with Mr Joerg, the Swiss Consul in Tientsin, who was then on his way to visit the camp at Weihsien.

That night we crossed the Yellow River bridge. It was brightly illuminated with floodlights and was heavily defended. The Japanese were very worried about their bridges on this line which had obviously been attacked many times. We frequently saw twisted girders beside the track and many bridges showed evidence of temporary repairs. Spare girders lay beside each of them. We also saw many shot up and abandoned engines in sidings, evidence of the continued aerial strafing to which the line was being subjected. We wondered what would happen if our own train were attacked and what would be the chances of making a run for it.

We still did not know where we were going but the word Fengtai was already being mentioned. No one knew very much about it, beyond the fact that it was a large railway junction and storage depot. Tungchow, to the east of Peking, also had many advocates and sounded a better place to go. At least if we were going there we should probably not be going to Japan.

Towards dusk on the evening of the fourth day, our doubts were resolved when we pulled into the station at Fengtai, and were ordered to detrain. What a sorry looking crew we were! Three nights without sleep and little chance to wash after our labours in packing and loading had left us looking more dead than alive. Many could hardly stand on their swollen feet and we had one genuine casualty in the person of Ralph Shaw who was in a high dysenteric fever and had spent the last twenty-four hours on a stretcher in an empty goods van, looked after by the Japanese medical orderlies. Our other invalids had stood the journey surprisingly well, thanks to the unexpectedly cooler weather.

We were told to dump all our hand baggage on the platform and that trucks would be sent for it later. We ourselves would have to walk. I asked if the trucks might not also carry the older men and the invalids. Honda then had to admit that he did not know when the trucks would be sent and that the sick would have to walk with the rest, all except Shaw for whom he would make arrangements later. Practically nobody was willing to leave his hand baggage containing his most precious possessions on an unguarded railway platform for an indefinite period, so we all started to try to sort things out of the pile again with the idea of carrying it with us. Honda said that we had only about half a mile to go, and tired as we were we felt that we could lug our gear that far.

At this juncture, greatly to our surprise, Colonel Odera appeared. We had imagined him far away in Japan, and wondered if a new camp for POWs had been set up at Fengtai which we were to join. He and Honda then started to act tough, probably to impress the representatives of the local Gendarmerie who had arrived to supplement our own guard. We were hustled into a straggling column of fours and told to march. It was by now about ten o'clock at night and pitch dark. We disposed our gear about ourselves as best we might and started off, guarded on either side by a file of troops.

The road first wound its way through the ill-lit main street of a Chinese village. The going here was not too bad, we could at least see each other, if only dimly. It was far otherwise after we left the few shop lights behind us and straggled through the outlying streets. Every China hand knows that the back streets of a Chinese village are not the pleasantest places in which to walk, even in broad daylight. In the dark, unfamiliar with the route, tired out and overburdened, it was a mild form of torture.

Here too, the guard began to show their true colours. They had not been gentle with the laggards in the lighted part of the route, but here in the dark they felt that they could make all the play with gun butts and muzzles that their hearts desired. Here also, I should record the fact that several of them who had come with us from Shanghai, after a hurried look round to make sure that their fellows should not perceive their weakness, took over and carried for the rest of the journey the baggage of men who had obviously reached the end of their tether.

Every ten minutes or so we were allowed a brief halt without which we could never have made the end of the journey. Honda's half mile had long been forgotten, although not the fact that he had once again lied to us to our very great discomfort. We left the village, then traversed country roads and then open fields before we finally arrived at at dimly lit guard house with a high wall stretching away into the darkness on either side. The total distance we had had to cover was probably not more than three miles but it had taken us the best part of two hours. We still had another quarter mile to go until we reached warehouses, known in China as godowns, which were to be our future home.

The accommodation provided for us had plain brick floors with a single straw mat for each man. It looked pretty good to us at the time. There was room to lie flat and to stretch out and that, for the moment, was all that we craved.

It was then I realized that Shaw was still at the station. I hunted up Honda and asked about the promised transport. Nothing doing, no trucks to be had, all drivers had gone to sleep. He agreed, however, to my trying to raise a carrying party to go down to the station and fetch Shaw back on a stretcher. I hated to do it. Everyone was dead beat. I should like to remember the names of the twelve men who volunteered to come back with me. I remember taking Pitts because he was big, and Winkleman because he could never be kept out of an extra job. Endo came too.

We stumbled back to the station and found Shaw somewhat better but still too weak to walk. We were selecting a few of the lighter medical packages to carry back with us when to our great relief a truck turned up. We loaded Shaw aboard with all the medical stores that were to hand, and a few bags of food, and sent him back to the camp with four men to look after him. The rest of us trudged back again over the long three miles for the last time that night. At the gate another surprise awaited us. A couple of the guards had saved a basin of hot soup apiece for us.

It must have been nearing 4 a.m. by the time we finally lay down on our strip of matting, asleep before we were properly stretched out. But not for long.

Shortly after six one of the guards shook me by the shoulder telling me to get up.

'What's the matter? What's all the hurry?'

'Must get up. Unload train very quickly.'

'Unload train?' said I, still fuddled.

'Yes, must unload by twelve o'clock.'

This thoroughly aroused me. 'But that's rubbish. I don't suppose I have a dozen men who can walk, let alone work, and it would take me until midday to get them down to the station, and as for unloading the train, quite impossible. Tell Honda I said so.'

'Oh no. Train very near, just behind camp. You come outside door and you can see.'

He was right. During the night the train had been shunted on to a siding parallel to and not more than 150 yards from the building in which we had passed the night. I suppose our little walk from the station had been their idea of a good joke.

21

FENGTAI

NOW for the first time, we were able to see our premises by daylight and to take stock of our surroundings. Our building was the first in a long line of enormous warehouses stretching far into the distance. Fronting us, at a distance of about one hundred and fifty yards was a similar row of warehouses but separated from us by a road and a line of barbed wire, fitted with insulators so that it could be electrified. For some unexplained reason, the kitchen was a quarter of a mile down the road, beside the guard house at the main gate. All food had to be transported thence to our quarters, but fortunately there was a light railway running along the side of the road, and we were able to borrow a few trucks to use on it.

Ordinarily the job of unloading the wagons would not have been much of a task. I was doubtful, however, whether we could get together enough fit men to make a real impression on the job. The only thing to do was to fall in the whole crowd, and then get Dr Sturton to walk down the lines, falling out those who were unfit for work. This proved to be a popular move, particularly as Sturton showed no mercy on those who had successfully malingered in the past, when labour was a surplus commodity. Everybody was suprisingly cheerful. We had at least arrived somewhere, it was a nice bright sunny day, too bright as it proved, and whatever was happening to us, at least it was a change from the humdrum routine of Haiphong Road.

The actual unloading was quickly done, but transport thence to our godowns was not so easy. The light railway served us for only part of the distance, and some of our stores were extremely heavy. We had about forty sacks of wheat and beans left, some weighing up to two hundred and thirty pounds. There were about ten of us left who could still take these on our shoulders as a one man load, which was the easiest means of handling them, but that trip, involving a stretch along loose brick and rubble, was definitely something to remember.

Somehow or other the job was done by five o'clock. The last task of the day was to return the trucks to the far end of the compound. Three of us did this, escorted by Endo. I went along to try to learn a little more of our surroundings. I had noticed that about every two hundred yards there was a stand pipe and a water trough. They were about a yard square, so I asked Endo if we might not stop at one of them to get a wash. The water was beautifully clear and cold, coming from an artesian well. After a careful look up and down the road, he suggested that we might even like to take a bath. The tanks were about three feet deep and was that bath marvellous! Apart from the fact that we were hot, dirty and tired, it was the first time that we had been completely immersed in water since we had left our homes nearly three years before.

Whilst the unloading had been going on, arrangements had been made for the allocation of the available living space. We had been given two compartments of a warehouse, each measuring about 80 by 170 feet. We decided to put about two hundred men in one compartment, and one hundred in the other, leaving half a compartment for the medical and dental clinics, carpenters and plumbers, office and space for the distribution of food. We tried hard to get extra space, and although there was plenty available, the Japanese would never allow us more.

The barbed wire surrounding us ran thirty feet from our east doors, and twenty-five from those on the south. Our free walking space was therefore extremely limited. There was no water inside this tiny compound, apart from a large emergency tank for use in case of fire. All water had to be brought in by buckets from a hydrant on the road outside the wire. Fetching water was not a popular job owing to the large amount of bowing involved. One had to bow to the sentry to get permission to go out and then bow again on the way in. Even the sentries got tired of being bowed to all day long by a constant stream of men, but instead of disposing with this useless formality they insisted on the men waiting until there was a bunch of ten or so, ready to go out or come in, and they would then have to line up and bow solemnly in unison.

There was no wash place provided. At first we would all go out to the hydrant to wash. Then they decided that this made it all too difficult to keep track of us so provided timber with which to make a rough bench and a few strips of matting for a rough screen. When the matting blew down, nobody bothered very much, but the Japanese were very indignant at the indecent exposure involved. Three Japanese women used to arrive daily to work in the building opposite and they seemed frightened of offending their tender susceptibilities. To us the latrine was the worst problem because it was open trench within twenty feet of our eating, sleeping, and living quarters. No chloride of lime or other disinfectant was provided, and when it rained, the trench overflowed.

We soon found evidence of the fact that the prisoners of war from the Kiangwan Camp in Shanghai had been there before us. This took the form of inscriptions here and there on the walls, behind doors, and in other obvious places. It was clear that they had been even more crowded than us. One such inscription read: 'Three hundred men of the 4th United States Marines lived here'. Another said: 'Prisoners of War from Shanghai left here for Japan on 12 June 1945'. We also found in one of the other compartments of our godown a large pile of stores which they had not been allowed to take. Many of these were things we could have made very good use of, but we were not allowed to touch them. This is not to say that none of them came into our possession. A week or so after we arrived we received a visit from a Japanese officer, a favourite with the Colonel, who told us he had accompanied the Shanghai POWs on their journey to Japan as part of their guard and that all had arrived safely. We always called him 'The Monk'. He had relieved Honda for a short period at Haiphong Road and had endeared himself to us by paying no attention to us whatsoever. On one occasion when there had been an air raid at night and the Quartermaster had asked for orders to put us through the usual drill, he had been heard to say 'No, let them sleep'. That was all he appeared to do himself all day, with his feet cocked up on his desk, and he apparently regarded sleep as the most important thing in life.

Life in Fengtai was different from that in Shanghai in many ways. There was a fair amount of work getting settled in but after that there was relatively little to be done. There was hardly any work for carpenters or plumbers, and very little office work since we were not allowed to correspond with anybody, and could do no buying either for kitchen or canteen. On the other hand personal chores such as laundry and cleaning took considerably longer as did almost everything owing to the lack of almost every kind of facility or appliance. The change of atmosphere and scenery was doing everyone good. We even had a distant view of the hills surrounding Peking. I do not think that anyone was bored although we should undoubtedly have become so had we been there for any length of time.

We naturally started a garden, although the soil was far from promising. The air was far less humid than in Shanghai and consequently the temperature was much higher. In Shanghai we could work barefoot, but here the sandy ground became so hot in the afternoons as to be insupportable. We had been accustomed to working hatless and shirtless in Shanghai, and thought that we were about as sunburned as we could be. We found however that here we took on an even blacker hue.

Food was perhaps slightly better than in Shanghai. Vegetables were a little more plentiful and the meat was camel instead of water buffalo. One thing we badly missed was bread. Honda would provide flour but not yeast, even though there was a tall chimney but a mile distant that belonged to a brewery. Bill Carr and his Corporal said that they had a little bakery experience so they were given the job of biscuit making. They tasted very good to us and were improving all the time. A couple of sacks of kaolin flour were delivered to us by mistake. I thought it might make a welcome change as breakfast porridge, so I got Buck Taylor to try grinding a few pounds in our stone mill and then had the idea of giving a little to the biscuit makers. It worked wonders in improving the shortness of the dough, which had always been a serious problem in view of our lack of adequate supplies of fat.

These were little things, but experiment and improvization were very literally the breath of life to us, apart from the sheer interest of it and the joy of achievement.

We had another big row with the Japanese at about this time. Our godown had a corrugated iron roof and since the temperature during the day would rise to something over 140 degrees the temperature inside was also pretty fierce. It was particularly insupportable at night when the breeze dropped and everyone had to be inside. Each compartment had large double doors at each end, but only those at the front were in use. There was a high barbed wire fence four feet from the rear doors and behind that a mud rampart of equal height on which sentries patrolled during the night. There were moreover lamps on high standards in the fields well behind the rampart so that these rear doors were well illuminated. One would have thought that under the circumstances, and with all these safeguards, there would have been no objection to these rear doors being opened during the night in order to alleviate somewhat the suffocating heat to which we were subjected. I offered to give a camp parole that no one would go through the doors, and that I would moreover so festoon them with barbed wire that no one could possibly get through them. The Japanese doctor himself protested to Honda, but all to no avail. It was totally unnecessary cruelties of this kind that really made us hate Honda and all that he represented. Necessary hardships we could take, but this kind of thing was just plain sadism.

A few weeks after we arrived we had three young Italians attached to us. They had belonged to the Italian Marine Legation Guard and had simply demobilized themselves when Italy officially dropped out of the war after the fall of Rome. They had been left alone until a few weeks previously, when the Gendarmerie had rounded them up and put them in cells.

Our next arrivals were much more to our liking. I had been told by Honda that we were to receive three or four men but that they would probably not be accommodated with us although he would like us to arrange to feed them. A day or so later we saw three bearded figures plodding along the road towards the Japanese office, their hands bound behind them, and tied to each other by ropes around their necks. I thought that they must be Chinese criminals whom I had frequently seen marched through the streets thus bound. They turned out to be United States Air Force pilots, headed by Captain Everett. They had all been shot down at various places and times during recent months, and for the last few weeks had been held in solitary confinement in Peking. There the Gendarmerie had been trying to extract information from them by the usual means.

One of them was in a very bad shape with dysentery and was allowed to be put into our camp hospital. The other two were put into No. 5 section of our building where they were, in theory, kept incommunicado. As we were feeding them, and had to take along the food and collect the empty dishes, we soon lapped up their news. Their arrival made us feel that we were definitely due shortly for Japan, since it appeared that our camp was being made a collecting centre for the area. One item of their news that interested us greatly was a rumour that had reached them through the prison grapevine in Peking to the effect that the Gendarmerie still held in solitary confinement there survivors of the famous Doolittle raid on Japan.* There had been four but one had recently died as a result of the terrible hardships they had undergone. This information proved useful later on.

We were getting very little news but had the feeling that the Japanese

---

* The Doolittle raid was a bombing mission commanded by Brigadier General James N. Doolittle of the US Army Air Force. On 18 April 1942, 16 B25s set out from the aircraft carrier *Hornet* and struck Tokyo, Yokahama, and other Japanese cities before proceeding westward, where most of the crews arrived safely behind friendly Chinese lines. The raid, renowned for its daring and success, greatly bolstered US morale.

were becoming distinctly jittery. The first open sign was the disarming of the Korean section of the garrison. There was a lot of bugle blowing and shouting in the building opposite to us one night and lights were kept burning until dawn. The next morning there were very few troops on parade. In the evening they were all back, but we noticed that half of them were unarmed. Knowing that the Koreans had every reason to be disaffected, we gathered that the Japanese must be fearing a landing in Korea and were taking precautions accordingly.

Apparently the Japanese were very short of guards for the compound with the virtual loss of these effectives, but they thought they might as well make some use of them. So they got half a dozen of them to make a forge down near our kitchen where they were set to work forging spearheads out of short lengths of soft iron, which were then bound to bamboo poles. These were the new and approved arms for the Koreans, since the Japanese felt they could not be trusted with firearms!

A few days after this, as a further evidence of their attack of jitters, the garrison started to build rifle pits all round our wire perimeter and not more than fifty yards from our doors. I asked Honda what it was all about and he said that there were believed to be large bands of communists in the neighbourhood and that this was being done for our 'protection'.

During the next few days the garrison embarked on an intensive programme of training, which was staged, mainly for our benefit, on the parade ground opposite us. All day long they did mock attacks, bayonet fighting and sword drill, all to the accompaniment of what were intended to be awe-inspiring screams. But the Japanese voice is too high-pitched when raised thus to be anything but rather funny.

22

THE SURRENDER

THERE was nothing in the dawn of 12 August to presage the momentous events of the day that followed. Although our news of world events had been scanty, we had been kept fairly well advised since our arrival in Fengtai of what went on in the Japanese office. A few months before we left Shanghai, there had been one of the periodic changes in the personnel of the guard. Among the newcomers was a youth of Formosan origin who had got into contact with our cook house staff. After feeling his way for a bit he told them that his parents were both Chinese who had emigrated to Formosa (Taiwan) and that consequently he regarded himself as Chinese rather than Japanese. He further said that he would like to help us if he could. No particular reliance was placed on these statements. There were too many stool-pigeons around the place for us to take any chances. It was up to him to show us that he meant it in some concrete form before we could place any trust in him. Little opportunity for him to demonstrate his good faith occurred before we left Shanghai.

In Fengtai he began to show up. His contact was now narrowed down to one man in the kitchen, Taffy Davies, who had taken pains to cultivate him. He now began to pass on to us scraps of information that he picked up through listening in to telephone conversations, and glancing at dispatches. Late on the morning of the 12th, he passed word to Taffy that an announcement had been made over the radio that at noon sharp, a pronouncement of the greatest importance would be made over the air from Tokyo by a very exalted personage. No one had the slightest idea what it was all about.

At midday, the guard turned out, formed up in line facing east, bowed three times and then remained at attention until dismissed. We wondered greatly at this unusual ceremony, but had no inkling as to its import. The guard, of course, being fully engaged in making obeisance in the open, had no opportunity to listen to the broadcast. It was not until dusk was falling that Taffy came up to me in a state of high excitement.

The Formosan had just got through to him and told him that the radio broadcast had been made by the Emperor himself announcing that the war was ended and all fighting was to cease immediately. Taffy had told no one else in case it should not be true, and had arranged a further meeting with the Formosan for later that evening to try to obtain further information.

This was tremendous news. Like Taffy, I could hardly credit it, and dared not broadcast the information. I got hold of Wright, Hopkins and Liddell, told them the story, and we agreed that we must keep it quiet until we were quite sure that it was true. If it should prove to be true, then we should have to take the utmost care to avoid any demonstration from our side or any action which might provoke the Japanese. We were a thousand miles from the nearest Allied troops who might take many weeks to reach us. There were probably half a million Japanese troops in North China, the majority of whom had not yet fired a shot in the defence of the fatherland, and our experience with them was not such as to lead us to place any reliance on their good faith, or in their observance of the rules of warfare.

At nine, Taffy had a further talk with the Formosan, but had not been able to glean any further news, other than reiteration of the original statement. All the camp offiers had left and were believed to have gone to Peking to Headquarters. A little later, the news was all round the camp in substantially the same form. We traced its origin back, and found that it came from one of the Korean guards, via 'Trooper' Watson. There was no point in further concealment so we called a hurried Captains' Meeting, told them what we also had heard in confirmation, and that although there appeared to be grounds for believing that the report was probably correct, we thought that it should still be treated with some reserve. We further emphasized, with all fully agreeing, that if it should prove to be true, we should have to watch our step very carefully indeed, and that all should co-operate to restrain any provocative act on the part of our irresponsible hot-heads. We well knew by now the ones that we should have to watch. The next few days might well prove to be the most critical and dangerous of the whole period of our imprisonment, and having come safely through so far, we wanted to be alive and kicking at the finish.

This may sound unduly apprehensive, but our attitude and precautions turned out to be fully justified. Honda admitted later during interrogation that they had seriously discussed whether or not they should kill us all and then commit hara-kiri themselves.

For hours that night excited groups of men stood about under the light of one dim bulb, high in the roof, debating in whispers the amazing news in all its aspects. Finally all were in bed, but not asleep. The news was too big, too upsetting, particularly to the internal organs. Never in my life have I heard such a succession of explosive rumbles, indicative of extreme intestinal disturbance.

The following morning we paraded as usual for roll-call at eight o'clock. The attitude of the Japanese at this routine ceremony might well give us the answer we hoped for. Our usual practice was to sound the precautionary call a few minutes before eight, when the men would fall in in roll-call order. We would then stand at ease awaiting the appearance of the inspecting officer from the door of the Japanese office on the far side of the road. The bugle would then blow the fall in, we would come to attention, and roll-call would be on.

The bugler blew the precautionary call and we lined up. For ten minutes nothing happened. This was distinctly encouraging. 'Blow again.' Still nothing. Then Endo appeared. He had never before taken roll-call, being too junior in rank. Then we knew definitely that something quite extraordinary had occurred, even if it might not be all that we hoped. He took roll-call in a very apologetic manner, but offered no explanation as to why he was doing so.

I do not know how we got through the rest of that day. No further news came through, although the Formosan spent all his time with his ear glued to the partition which separated him from the one official telephone.

The officers were rarely in evidence, and then only coming or going in a cloud of dust. It was not until the following morning that definite confirmation was obtained.

Honda sent for me.

'Good morning, Mr Collar. Have you heard the news?'

'What news, Lieutenant?'

'You mean you do not know anything?'

'Anything about what, Lieutenant?'

There was no point in letting him know we did know, which would simply provoke questions as to how we knew, and our sources of information might still be valuable to us.

'Then I must explain everything to you. We are informed that negotiations are going on between the Japanese and American governments with a view to putting an end to further unnecessary fighting. We understand that the American government has submitted certain proposals to His Imperial Japanese Majesty's government which we are now considering. No information has been received since the original announcement but we understand that negotiations are not yet completed and are still going on. Of course nothing may come of it and our government may reject the terms of the American government. In the meantime, however, I have received orders from the High Command to do everything possible to make you more comfortable. Will you please let me know what are your wishes?'

I cannot possibly convey to you the impression made by this bald statement. Delivered in poor English, with many hesitations, and with much hissing, it told me all that we wanted to know. What did we want to make us comfortable!

In little over half an hour I was back with Honda carrying our list of wants which included everything we knew they had stock of but were withholding, and a great deal more besides. He took it and glanced through it without batting an eyelid. In addition, I told him that we did not want any more Japanese supervised roll-calls. We would give them a daily report in future, signed by myself and Wright. We wanted much greater freedom of movement for the men within the confines of the camp until such time as we came to leave. With a view to avoiding unpleasant incidents we wished all contact between internees and guards to be minimized and we requested that he give appropriate orders to his own men as we would to ours.

Endo was soon across with the list. He was the only one who would come near us now. He took us into the store and in effect said, 'Help yourselves'.

It was a little later in the day that I got an inkling of what had happened. I was talking to Endo, trying to get a clearer picture of the situation. He was definite that Japan had surrendered to the Allied Forces, and said that there was some mention of an atom bomb that none of them could quite understand, although they were clear that it was something pretty dreadful.

The garrison had hitherto been little in evidence, but now they resumed their morale building exercises with even greater vigour than before. They slaved away in front of us from morning till night. They might be either working the troops hard so that they had no time to think, or else they were working them up to a state of frenzy and blind obedience. We did not feel that we were out of the woods yet.

23

THE TABLES ARE TURNED

ON the 15th I was told that a further eight or ten men would be coming to the camp that day, and was asked to prepare for them. In the evening Wright, Hopkins, Capt. Everett and I were sent for by the Colonel. When we arrived in his room we found with him Commander Cunningham, USN, former Commander of Wake Island, whom I had last seen in Ward Road Gaol in the summer of 1942, where he had been confined with Lt.-Commander Smith, USN, and Commander Wolley, RN, following their unsuccessful attempt to escape from the POW camp at Woosung.

The Colonel produced a bottle of brandy and we all had one with Cunningham, before escorting him back to our quarters where the other men of his escape party were already being fed and cared for.

He was somewhat dazed. He told us that three hours earlier he had had no idea whatever that the war was over and indeed little knowledge of its progress. He had been standing in his cell waiting for seven o'clock when he could sit down. We did not quite understand what he meant by this until he explained that he was forced to stand for ten hours a day, in his solitary confinement cell. He had been in solitary practically the whole time since the failure of his attempted escape from the Shanghai gaol in 1943. During this time he had undergone practically every form of torture that the Japanese could devise. His men were amazed that any one man could take what he had taken and still live, and they were full of the deepest admiration for him.

I do not think that any of them slept much that night. Sleep was the last thing they wanted. They wanted most of all to appreciate the savour of being once again free men among friendly people, and to be able to talk as loudly and as long as they wished. They seemed to be absolutely inexhaustible, and we had to arrange for relays of listeners, not that there was any lack of eager audiences.

It may have been the same day or on the next day that at about three in the afternoon a B29 circled low over the camp and then flew off in the direction of Peking where it vanished behind the hills. We waved our home-made flags, and set out camp beds to form a big V, but could not detect any answering signal from the plane. I had just gone inside when men shouted that it had reappeared in the direction of Peking and was dropping parachutes. I was talking to Capt. Everett at the time and we went out together in time to see the last of the chutes coming down. He said that from their colour they were supply-dropping parachutes and we wondered what on earth they could be dropping. It is a pity that he had not seen the earlier ones, or that nobody had particularly noticed that they were different in colour, or we should have known that men had been dropped first.

We did hear rumours on the following day that some American officers had arrived in Peking but it was not until we arrived in Peking that we heard their story. Eight men came in all, under the command of Major Wheeler. Only one of them had made a parachute jump before, and they chose to make their first ever jump bang into the middle of half a million very recent ex-enemies, without prior notification, and therefore without any indication as to what the reaction of these ex-enemies would be. For sheer cold nerve, I think that takes a lot of beating. They demanded to be put immediately into touch with the C.-in-C. of the Japanese North China Forces. Just like that! A startled Chief of Staff met them and from then on what happened was in the lap of the Gods. Very fortunately for us, the C.-in-C. accepted the situation and agreed to co-operate, but Major Wheeler had to tread very delicately. His careful mixture of tact and firmness was admirable and achieved the measure of success that it deserved. One of his first actions was to request that we, and all other military or civilian prisoners in that part of China be brought immediately to Peking where they could be centralized under his immediate care. Unfortunately we did not find this out until we met him in Peking.

The day following the arrival of the parachutists, Honda called me to go to his office and said I probably knew that the premises in which we were now quartered would be very cold and uncomfortable during the winter and that he had accordingly been doing his utmost to find more suitable accommodation. After a laborious search, he had now discovered some very suitable premises, to which he proposed we should move immediately, immediately being at seven o'clock the following morning.

This was a bit of a facer. We definitely did not want to make any hurried move. Our existing quarters would do nicely for the autumn months, when the North China climate is at its best, but we especially did not want to move from a location which we were satisfied was known to the Allied Forces, and arrive in some unspecified region where they might have difficulty in finding us. This we would have resisted to the uttermost.

A few days earlier, the altered situation had caused us to make a change in our governing organization. We felt that each nation should now be more directly represented in the higher councils and we had accordingly formed a new committee comprising Hopkins for the Americans, Kreulen for the Dutch, Kalafatis for the Greeks, and Wright and myself for the British. I refused to discuss Honda's proposals further without the presence of the full committee. Honda did not like this. He much preferred to talk to me alone. It is much easier to give an order to one unfortunate and to leave him to bear the brunt of seeing it carried out, than to argue with an unfriendly crowd. I was not having any of that and insisted on fetching them.

We had a marvellous and typical Honda argument, lasting until nearly midnight. He simply could not understand why we were not properly appreciative of the tremendous effort that he had been putting forth on our behalf. His sole motive was to try to make us more comfortable in accordance with orders received from High Command. He simply did not understand why we kept saying that we did not want to be made more comfortable and that all we now wanted of the Japanese was to be supplied with food and left alone. Unfortunately he could not give us a description of these very attractive premises that he had found for us, and it was pretty evident that he had neither seen them, nor even knew exactly where they were. We asked if it was his idea of loving care to order us to move at seven the following morning, which would mean waking up the men now asleep and spending the whole night packing. Well, accommodation was very scarce and we had to snap it up whilst we could, and so on *ad nauseam*. Not once during the whole argument did he say that there was an American rescue team in Peking and that they had asked that we should be brought to them immediately.

I finally suggested that since we seemed to be unable to come to an agreement he should refer the matter to the Colonel whom I felt sure would appreciate the reasonableness of our attitude. After some demur Honda did so, and rather to our surprise came back with the Colonel's consent to drop the matter.

Wright and I were rather pleased with the evening, not so much because Honda had been bested, but because it had given the others an opportunity of seeing for themselves just what an argument with

Honda could be like. I thought that would be the last we should hear of the argument and wondered idly why the Colonel sent for me shortly after lunch on the following day. Commander Cunningham and Capt. Everett were already with him. He chatted idly with us for a few minutes and then gently, oh so gently, came back to the same old topic. As soon as he got properly started, and I realized that it was not just idle conversation but a definite reopening of the whole matter, I said, as I had done with Honda, that I was not prepared to discuss it without the remainder of the committee being present. The Colonel retorted that this was entirely unnecessary and that we could decide the matter very well without them. Fortunately he was called away to the telephone, and whilst he was out I nipped back and fetched the crowd. Then the whole argument started again, still without mention whatsoever of the American rescue party.

It went on for the best part of two hours when it became obvious that we were getting nowhere and that the Colonel was on the point of blowing up completely. It was Hopkins who finally brought matters to a head by saying:

'The position is that we are not willing to move and that if you wish us to move you can only make us do so by using force. Is it your intention to use force if necessary?'

'YES', said the Colonel and stalked out of the room with none of that show of politeness which had hitherto veneered the conversation.

I shall always admire Hopkins for that. It took a lot of courage to face up to the Japanese when you had been under their heel for so long, and the Colonel was clearly in a very explosive state.

So, move it was and by eight o'clock that night. Another tremendous scurry, but our recent training made it a much more expeditious job this time. We were told that we should be accommodated in two buildings in Peking, just across the street from each other. We arranged that I should go with the first convoy and attend to unloading and billeting in the new premises, whilst Bill Wright would remain behind to complete the packing and despatch at the camp.

The first convoy of a dozen heavily loaded trucks got away soon after eight and shortly after dusk started to rumble through the streets of Peking. I was in the leading truck and was therefore past the crowds in the streets before they realized that there was anything unusual about this particular convoy. Then they began to get it and the roar of cheers was tremendously heartening.

Our accommodation was not half bad, being a Japanese-style hotel that was clean, adequately supplied with showers and toilets, and obviously well cared for. Shortly after we arrived it began to rain in torrents. I enquired about the premises for the other half of the camp so that I could go across and begin to get ready to receive them. Nobody had the least idea where it was, not only that, but I could not go there anyway. We were, of course, still under Japanese guard and could not move without permission. I was completely helpless and had to leave the others to get on as best they could. They had a terrible time. Both they and their stores were drenched, and when they arrived in their hotel, which was nearly two miles from ours, they found the roof leaking in a dozen places and half the rooms uninhabitable. I felt really guilty when I was able to visit them the following morning and compare their wretched accommodation with ours.

It was not until that afternoon that Major Wheeler was able to visit us. He came accompanied by the Colonel, Honda and an Aide to the C.-in-C. After a quick word of greeting and a look at the premises, Major Wheeler gathered the inspection party into a small lounge, which was fortunately well provided with windows so we were able to stand and hear the show.

This was the Colonel and Honda being put through it, particularly Honda. He stood there grey faced and sweating. They were put through a rapid-fire barrage of questions on us and their treatment of us. The questioning turned to Hutton. How he had died, when he had died, where he had died, what had been done with his body? Cremated, eh. Wasn't that very convenient, didn't leave any evidence, did it? Question followed question, insistent, demanding, no face slapping, no water cure, but Honda was going through it just the same. There were so many questions to which he had no answers. He had records, hadn't he? Where were they? They must be produced immediately. Honda got no relief until Major Wheeler's questions turned to the three Doolittle survivors and to the one recently reported dead, about whom we had been able to tell him. These were not in Honda's province but in that of the local Gendarmerie, a representative of which was produced by the Japanese Aide who was also looking very uncomfortable indeed. More rapid-fire questions, and a grudging admission that they were in custody in Peking. Immediate orders that they be produced within the hour. Then the one lately dead. What had he died of, when had he died, what disposal had been made of the body? Orders again that the body must be produced for examination.

This was particularly fortunate for the body. It was that of Lt. Barr who turned out not to be dead at all although not very much alive. He was brought to the Peking Hotel, on the top floor of which we had set up our hospital. He was suffering terribly from dysentery, beri-beri, and neglect. He was eventually pulled round and was indirectly the means of obtaining my own early release.

That was about all for the day. Major Wheeler was up to the eyes in work and clearly wanted us to look after ourselves as far as we could for a day or two whilst he assured himself that he had located and brought in all missing prisoners in the neighbourhood. He had a pile of K Rations sent round to us and promised more when the next plane came in. I rather gather that K Rations were not exactly popular with the American Army. You did not hear any of us complain.

The next day I felt that the war really had ended. Major Wheeler had not had time to go to the other hotel but I had told him that it was badly in need of repair and that it was completely lacking in cooking facilities. Our protests to the Japanese had not yet borne fruit. On that next morning I was invited into the office of the Japanese officer who was now in charge of our guard, and there introduced to two officers of an engineering unit.

Their first words to me were: 'Mr. Collar, please tell us what are your orders.'

We had by now managed to have the guard removed out of our hotel altogether, although they still remained on duty at the gate. Although we were not now subject to their orders, they had requested through Major Wheeler that we should not go on to the streets except for essential purposes. The town was still full of troops whose temper was distinctly uncertain, and the Japanese troops were responsible for our safety, until such time as we should be removed or the Americans could bring in adequate policing forces.

Later that day a B29 flew in with more supplies, and took in it on the return journey all the servicemen with us, including Commander Cunningham, Capt. Everett, and the Doolittle men with the exception of Lt. Barr who was too ill to be moved.

The day before they left, I accompanied Commander Cunningham, Capt. Everett, two of Major Wheeler's staff, and a party of Japanese officers to the site of our late camp on a visit of inspection. Colonel Odera and Honda were there awaiting us. I had not been invited to this party, but when I heard of it, I knew that it was something I could not afford to miss. If it was, as I assumed, to be a visit of inspection, there was a great deal that I could tell that was not known to either Cunningham or Everett. I thoroughly enjoyed that trip.

The Colonel showed the party round with an air of a custodian, proudly displaying the jewels of the crown. An army of men must have been at work since we left, cleaning, and tidying up. I cannot pretend that we left the place in anything but a horrible mess, so rapid had been our departure, but there was more to it than just tidying up after the late tenants. It had obviously been prepared as carefully as possible for just this inspection.

It was ostensibly being prepared for the reception of Japanese refugees from the Kalgan area. Blankets and comfort boxes were neatly laid out in rows on the floor, and the Colonel remarked that, as could be seen from the notices on the door, they were preparing to put two hundred and fifty people in one compartment, whereas we had complained of overcrowding with two hundred. I was then able to show the inspecting party the inscriptions on the walls, left behind by the American and British POWs to the effect that there had been three hundred of them in each. Moreover there had been no blankets and comfort boxes awaiting us on arrival although they could apparently produce them at a moment's notice for their own people.

And so it went all the way round. When Odera proudly displayed the handsome toilet accommodation, by now complete with roof, I told how that roof had been hastily put on by the Japanese NCOs themselves on the afternoon of our departure, having failed to get us to break off our packing to do it for them. Then I took them to the site of the open trenches which had served us for the majority of our time. It didn't matter what the Colonel said, I was always ready with a contradiction or correction. I really did enjoy that little outing. It was the last time I saw Colonel Odera and Honda, and I think by then they were equally glad to see the last of me.

24
HOMEWARD BOUND

A FEW days after the departure of Commander Cunningham and Captain Everett, I was informed that two supply planes would be landing the following day and would be taking back Lt. Barr and exchanging some of Major Wheeler's personnel. There would be room on these planes for some thirty of us, and Major Wheeler would like me to prepare a list of the men whose presence in Shanghai was most urgently needed. Both Hopkins and I had been urging on him the need to get a substantial number of us to Shanghai as rapidly as possible. There were many men with us who occupied key positions in important undertakings there, such as utilities, shipping, banks, and so on, and every man who had a business of any kind that had been taken over and operated by the Japanese was anxious to get back as rapidly as possible in order to prevent them having a last fling at the disposal of remaining assets and at the concealment or destruction of the records of what they had been doing during these past years.

This really was a vital matter, both for the community at large and for the individuals whose businesses were at stake. Major Wheeler was immediately sympathetic and had asked Kunming to provide the requisite transport as soon as possible. These two planes appeared to be the first answer to our prayer. I was asked to produce the list within an hour. This precluded the possibility of consultation since the only committee that works fast is a committee of one. I knew that the only person who would really wholeheartedly approve of my selection would be the ones selected and this meant that I should have to leave myself off it to face the music, particularly as many of those who had hitherto taken a prominent part in the management of our camp affairs would be included. I could not well leave the camp entirely without experienced guidance, even if the war was over.

The next morning, in the middle of the excited packing of the fortunate thirty, a message arrived to say that there had been some mistake and that the planes would have to return direct to Kunming whence transport to Shanghai was virtually impossible. I was further told that passages would be available on these planes to a like number of men who wished to leave China and that transport from Kunming to India could be provided.

I put a notice on the board to this effect and was surprised at the paucity of the applications. Of course most of the men had their families in Shanghai but even then, twelve was a very small number, including as it did four men whom I knew intended to take their chance on getting either to Shanghai or Hong Kong from Kunming. It was then that I decided that perhaps this was my chance. I could get up to Chungking from Kunming, press at Army Headquarters the claims of our key men for early transport to Shanghai, and at the same time cable to London to find out what ICI's ideas about my own personal movements were. If they wanted me back in Shanghai, I should probably be able to get there not much later than if I remained in Peking, and if they were willing for me to go straight on leave, which I fervently hoped would be the case, I should be well on my way.

I had many qualms about leaving. Although the war was now well and truly over and the situation in Peking *vis-à-vis* the Japanese appeared to be stabilized, I felt very much like a deserter. However, Major Wheeler, Hopkins, and Liddell, with whom I discussed the idea of the visit to Chungking, were very much in favour of it, so I decided to go. Both Hopkins and Liddell wrote long supporting letters to the American and British Embassies and Major Wheeler gave me pointers on whom to see at Army HQ.

The number of those who were to go was not settled until virtually the last minute. Lt. Barr was still in our hospital in the Peking Hotel. I had seen him the day before with Mark King, also a patient, who had been put in with him to provide cheerful companionship. There could have been no better choice. Mark was a born humorist and never without a joke, even in our blackest moments. Dr Sturton decided that no chances could be taken with Lt. Barr and that he should wait a little longer before leaving. His recovery already bordered on the miraculous and it would be the greatest of pities if anything should go wrong now.

I did not have time to go round and say goodbye to everyone, for which I was not really sorry. We had gone through so much together that leave-taking would have been a very trying business. Harold Aiers drafted me a farewell message, the last of many services which he had so efficiently carried out during the three years. At 8.30 a.m. on 29 August, therefore, I climbed onto a Japanese army truck for the last time and set out at top speed for the western airfield.

Two Dakotas were waiting at the airport. At 9.45 a.m. we were off the ground and flying over the gilded roofs of Peking for a last look. We headed first for Sian which we reached at 2 p.m. The aerodrome was a veritable sea of mud except for the landing strip itself, and it rained all that afternoon and night. We were found quarters in a rough barracks surrounded by liquid mud a foot thick. Here we had our first introduction to the way in which America feeds its soldiers, even in such an out of the way place as Sian where practically everything had to be brought in by air. It was fortunate that our food in Peking had been a little better than that to which we had been accustomed for so long, or the sudden transition would have upset our stomachs completely.

Our journey to Kunming took another six hours.

I think that we were the first load of rescued civilian internees to arrive. General Aurans himself was there to meet us and lent his own car to myself, Dr Leighton Steward, later to become US Ambassador to China, and a Chinese of whose name I have now no record, who was posing as his Chinese secretary. The latter had been acting for some time past as Chiang Kai Shek's personal representative in Peking and both he and Dr Leighton Stewart had been asked by the Generalissimo to come to Chungking to report on the North China situation. The three of us were therefore bound together by our common desire to get to Chungking as quickly as possible, and word to that effect had been passed on by Major Wheeler from Peking. Somehow this message must have gone astray. This was a load of would-be evacuees from China and as such we must and would be treated.

We were first sent off to a very pleasant little medical centre and given rooms and beds in the reception wing of the hospital. We were divested of our clothes and put into hospital pyjamas and dressing gowns. Our particulars were recorded, we three saying, as we had said at the airport, that this was very pleasant, but please, we wanted to go to Chungking. Yes, Yes, this is just a formality. It will give you something to do whilst you are waiting.

The particulars taken, we were directed to the X-ray department a little way down the road, and thence to the blood and stool testing clinic. We began to protest more volubly. What was being done to get us passages to Chungking? The nurses were charming but firm. Clearly we had been through great hardships and really did not know quite what we were saying. Colonel So-and-So always called in the evenings and we should tell our story to him. When he arrived he professed kindly interest but seemed to me to be far from convinced.

We had another arrival that evening. A Captain Huggett of the American Air Force. He had been flying fighter planes out of Clark Field and Bataan, and had escaped by native boat to Indo-China when Corregidor fell. There he had joined the French guerillas and had fought with them for many months before being captured by the Japanese. In prison camp he had managed to get hold of a radio which was smuggled in by American contacts still at large and had maintained contact between prison camp and the O.S.S. Since the prisoners were forced to work outside the camp he was able to pick up and pass on many valuable pieces of information. It was not until the end of 1944 that his usefulness decreased to the extent that he received permission to try to escape. This he did and then set out to walk to Kunming. It took him just under eight months to make the journey. The French Croix de Guerre was waiting for him when he arrived in Kunming that night. He was a sight to watch. He talked very little and that slowly and haltingly as though he had to familiarize himself again with his own language. He just sat quietly by himself for hours, so clearly enjoying the pleasure of just being able to sit and do nothing.

The next day we really met our Waterloo. We were aroused bright and early for breakfast but told to keep in our hospital clothes. We asked again about our transport to Chungking but received only vague replies. We were now regarded as definitely eccentric. After breakfast we were all herded into a long room. In this room were fourteen doctors, each with his little label and set of tools of his trade. First a form to be filled out, which gave us a further opportunity to protest that all this did not seem to be of any interest to us. We wanted to go to Chungking and would they please note that down on the form with the rest of the particulars. However there was nothing for it, we had to run the gauntlet of these fourteen doctors in order to get out of the room now that we were inside.

We then went through the sort of thing that I always imagine as being the prodecure at the Mayo Clinic. Every inch of our anatomy was searched and probed to make sure that we were fit to associate with humanity again. We even ended up with a psychoanalyst who had the nerve to ask me if I liked the Japanese and if not, why not. To receive final absolution and get out of the door, we had to be vaccinated, innoculated, and disinfected against half the known diseases in medical textbooks.

This was really the last straw for poor Dr Stewart. When a plane was arranged for him a few days later he was so knocked out by the many injections he had received that he was unable to travel.

That afternoon we were transferred to a rest camp some miles outside Kunming. There we remained for several days until the Americans decided that we British were really no concern of theirs and that we should properly be looked after by the British Consul, Mr Coghill. To the British Consulate we therefore moved. I sent cables to my wife in Canada and to my parents and the company in England and then started to press again for the passage to Chungking. I finally got away by RAF plane on 6 September. The journey was a nightmare for I was in agony from sciatica.

Was I pleased to see V. R. Butts when I arrived at the company's house in Chungking! Here I was at last in a home. Not a camp, or a barracks, but a home, with a servant in white clothes to bring a cup of tea and then to prepare a bath, and a real bed to sleep on, and clean clothes and well polished shoes to put on in the morning. No more bugles, no more morning parades, no more orders to give or receive. I was not yet at the end of the journey, but this felt like the first real evidence that I was well on my way.

During the next few days I called on the British Ambassador, Sir Horace Seymour, the Netherlands Ambassador, Mr E. Lovink, the American Embassy where I was unable to see General Patrick Hurley who was then away trying to compose the differences between the Kuomintang and the Communists, and the HQ of the American Army. To them all I told the same tale of the need to get as many of our men back to Shanghai in a hurry as possible, with special reference to those in key positions. Before I left I had the satisfaction of seeing a cable from Shanghai backing up my efforts and giving the names of those whose presence was most urgently required, and was told that immediate arrangements were being made to put the move into effect. The only thing that shook me about this cable was that my own name was included therein. I had just had a cable from London authorizing me to take immediate leave and to rejoin my family in Canada and had my passage already booked. I was never able to learn the precise origin of the former cable so I felt justified in ignoring it, as I very naturally wanted to do.

On 19 September I left Chungking by CNAC plane on the first leg of my long trip home. This was quite an eerie experience. The main aerodrome at Chungking was on a mud-flat in the middle of the river. This always flooded during the summer high-water season, and this was the first day it had been used since the water went down. I had to be at the aerodrome office on the top of the river bank an hour or so before dawn. We checked in at the office, and were then directed down a steep and completely unlit flight of stone steps. These twisted and turned and had it not been for the oil paper lanterns of the coolies carrying the baggage in front of us, we should not have been able to keep to the steps at all. The steps finally came to an end. By this time the lanterns were swaying about far to our right. We staggered and slipped along the muddy banks of the river with a roaring flood on our left and finally, after about half a mile of this, came to the place where the lanterns had halted. Here we found a sampan, held against the bank, into which we piled. The sampan pushed off into the stream, paddling frantically against the eight-knot current. We still could not see a thing but knew we were being swept rapidly downstream and hoped that we should strike the island before we found ourselves somewhere down in the Szechuen Gorges. We did, of course, just as dawn was breaking, and were carried pick-a-back through a foot of soft ooze. We took off at eight, and the leg to Calcutta was plain sailing. Here I lived in what seemed to me to be the height of luxury with R. Fraser Thompson of our India Company, whilst awaiting my flight to England. It was here I received the first of many cables from my wife, asking me in effect, if not in precise words, what the hell I was waiting for. She was no more impatient than I was.

The morning of 23 September saw me leaving Calcutta in a Sunderland flying boat operated by the BOAC with RAF personnel. Homeward via Karachi, Bahrain, and Cairo — where we passed the night very comfortably in a houseboat on the Nile.

The next leg of our journey nearly proved fatal.

The weather was fine and clear when we left Cairo, and after circling the Pyramids we struck off into the Mediterranean, setting course direct for Augusta in Sicily which was to be our stop for the night. We had been flying for about four hours when we ran into dense masses of cumulus cloud. They reached from practically sea level to well over 16,000 feet which was far above the ceiling of our comfortable but heavy Sunderland. The only thing to do therefore was to keep moderately low and weave a course around and about between the worst of them. This the pilot managed to do successfully for about an hour. Precisely what happened then I do not know, but I suspect that he turned round the edge of a cloud expecting to find a gap which was unfortunately not there. Certain it is that we went slap into the middle of a cumulus cloud of the worst type and immediately hit a collosal down-draft that shot us all straight out of our seats to the roof. It had been so unexpected that nobody had been strapped in. By the time I scrambled back into my seat and grabbed the table to hold myself in, we were in a vertical side-slip with an angry sea roaring its way up to us only a few hundred feet below. My face was pressed against the window beside me and even if I wanted to I could not have turned away. At long last, just when I had given up all hope that we should come out of it, the plane started to right itself and came back on to an even keel, a scanty fifty feet above the sea. As we hurriedly strapped ourselves in, the pilot fought his way back to higher altitudes. He had not been strapped in, and had been shot up to the roof just as we had been. Unfortunately his roof was cluttered with sharp instruments. His head had been quite badly cut and he was partially stunned. By the time he had shaken the blood out of his eyes and had found his way back to the controls we were well into the vertical side-slip which had so nearly been the end of us.

On the following morning we set out in the midst of a full gale on the last lap for home. It was the RAF crew's last flight too and they were as anxious to get back as we were. This was what so many of us had been waiting for, for so many years. I was the only one from China proper, but the rest were mostly ex-prisoners and internees from Stanley Camp in Hong Kong, from Changi Gaol in Singapore, and from the infamous Siam Railway. It was not to be the real end of my journey, I still had to cross to Western Canada, but England was for me the symbol, as it was to the others the actuality, the end of the journey.

We landed in the harbour at Poole in the soft light of an English summer evening. A motor boat conveyed us quickly to the quay and we thankfully and prayerfully climbed the wet stone steps to set our feet once more on English soil. Facing us at the top of the steps was a pub, the sort that we had dreamed of managing some day in our declining years. In the window was a notice. It said:

'SORRY. NO MORE BEER.'

INDEX

CHINA 1937

200 0 200 400 600 800 1000 km

++++ Shanghai — Peking Railway

Urumchi •

Chen

Kunming •

BURMA

FR
I
C

SIAM